Eye for
MASTERWORKS

Excellence
FROM WINTERTHUR

BY

DONALD L. FENNIMORE

AMANDA E. LANGE

ROBERT F. TRENT

DEBORAH E. KRAAK

E. McSHERRY FOWBLE

NEVILLE THOMPSON

PHOTOGRAPHY BY

GEORGE FISTROVICH

THE HENRY FRANCIS du PONT WINTERTHUR MUSEUM, INC.

WINTERTHUR, DELAWARE

1994

SPONSORS

Eye for Excellence: Masterworks from Winterthur is funded by
CHUBB GROUP OF INSURANCE COMPANIES,
FIDELITY INVESTMENTS THROUGH THE FIDELITY FOUNDATION,
and THE HENRY LUCE FOUNDATION, INC.

Front and back cover details from needlework by Mary King, 1754 (see p. 100).

Library of Congress Cataloguing-in-Publication Data
Henry Francis du Pont Winterthur Museum.
    Eye for excellence: masterworks from Winterthur/by Donald L.
Fennimore . . . [et al.].
    Includes bibliographical references.
    ISBN 0-912724-26-9
    1. Henry Francis du Pont Winterthur Museum—Catalogs.
2. Decorative arts—Delaware—Winterthur—Catalogs.   I. Fennimore,
Donald L.   II. Title.
NK460.W48H4545   1994
745′.0974′0747511—dc20   94-20001
                                                           CIP

CONTENTS

Eye for Excellence required the work of many hands, and numerous individuals merit special recognition. The planning and installation of the exhibition that this catalogue documents was a formidable task. Felice Jo Lamden, exhibition coordinator, guided the entire process with remarkable thoroughness. The talented conservation staff assessed the condition of every object in painstaking detail and then carried out the necessary treatments: Mark Anderson, Gregory Landrey, Michael Podmaniczsky (furniture); Margaret Little, Deborah Long, Julie Reilly (metalwork, glass, and ceramics); Betty Fiske, John Krill (prints, books, and manuscripts); Wendy Samet (paintings); Linda Eaton, Joy Gardiner, Lynne Hoyt, Susan Schmitt (textiles and embroidery). Students in the art conservation program assisted with several projects. Douglas MacDonald, art handling supervisor, oversaw the moving of objects through every phase. George Fistrovich produced the exceptional photographs. Grace Eleazer, associate registrar, coordinated all photography, and Wilbur Steltzer processed all orders. Onie Rollins, assistant editor, with Teresa Vivolo, copy editor, prepared the manuscript for publication.

Finally, the staff and trustees of Winterthur extend their deepest appreciation to the Chubb Group of Insurance Companies, Fidelity Investments through the Fidelity Foundation, and The Henry Luce Foundation, Inc. for their generous support.

Henry Francis du Pont opened the museum at Winterthur in 1951, the culmination of more than thirty years of zealous collecting. He had assembled his superlative collection of objects, made or used in America before 1840, with one purpose in mind: to found a museum documenting the work of early American artists and artisans. Few of the collecting fraternity in the United States at that time shared his enthusiasm for American decorative arts, preferring eighteenth-century English and French antiques instead. Du Pont believed passionately that American antiques were second to none and set out to form a comprehensive collection.

Fortunately, H. F. du Pont was active at a time when many great objects came to the market, and he was often able to acquire the most important. By the time of his death in 1969, the Winterthur collection included some 59,000 items and was widely considered to be the best in the world. It did not stop growing then, however. Believing that the collection would never be "finished," du Pont left instructions to the trustees of his estate and museum, listing numerous types of objects that had eluded him but which he hoped would eventually be acquired.

The museum professionals who have carried on the vision that du Pont established for Winterthur have researched and catalogued the collection, and they have added dramatically to its material and historical riches. The collection is not just a litany of the best of Anglo-, German, and Dutch American artistry and craftsmanship dating before the mid nineteenth century, however; it is also a profound educational tool that du Pont felt could provide accurate and telling insights into the lives of early Americans. Guests have enjoyed viewing the interiors assembled and furnished by du Pont, but they have also learned about life and living in early America. Scholars of American material culture have come not only to study but also to be trained in a graduate program founded by du Pont and co-sponsored by the University of Delaware.

My colleagues at Winterthur investigate the concept of masterwork in this catalogue and in the exhibition that it documents. In its simplest application, the term conveys that the maker of an object has mastered its medium, but the specific subtleties of the concept vary from culture to culture, time to time, and medium to medium. The objects illustrated and discussed here have been selected from the unparalleled riches of the Winterthur collection and all demonstrate not just mastery but also the infinite subtle variations inherent in a true masterwork.

Dwight P. Lanmon
Director

INTRODUCTION

INTRODUCTION

The phrases "treasure house of early American rooms," "a collection of America's finest antiques," and "a house which records the decorative history of our country" describe only one institution, Henry Francis du Pont's extraordinary creation at Winterthur.[1] With ardent care, scholarship, and energy, du Pont (1880–1969) transformed his family estate in the rolling hills of northern Delaware into a legendary landscape of naturalistic gardens complemented by a jewel box of historic interiors. *Eye for Excellence* celebrates the Winterthur collection, the fruits of more than seventy years of collecting the best of America's past.

Like many collectors, du Pont developed his own standards of excellence. He always insisted upon authenticity, frequently preferred a documented item to an undocumented one, and invariably took color, line, and appropriateness for a particular space into consideration. Architectural interiors and paneling found in buildings from New Hampshire to South Carolina formed the backdrop for his exceptional collection. The result emphasized harmony, balance, and order. Small details lent lively intimacy but never overwhelmed a room. Du Pont favored household objects used in America and, within these boundaries, concentrated on pieces made in the eighteenth and early nineteenth centuries.

In the quarter century since du Pont's death, a succession of Winterthur curators and conservators have sustained his passion for excellence, adding nearly 20,000 objects to the collection. Many items strengthen traditional areas of interest such as English glass and Philadelphia rococo furniture. Others broaden the scope of the collection. The recent purchase of green-glazed creamwares in the cauliflower pattern introduces a popular form of late eighteenth-century tableware that du Pont never chose to acquire. The extension of collecting limits from 1840 to 1860 has led to the addition of such forms as a flamboyant rococo revival chandelier and a gilt overmantel mirror. A commitment to document a greater diversity of cultures has spawned heightened interest in the contributions of Continental and African

American artisans as well as the achievements of Native Americans. Today the collection numbers nearly 80,000 objects and includes almost every form of domestic article used in America before the Civil War. An extensive library of 500,000 items documents the history of American material culture to 1920. These resources, in the words of Henry Francis du Pont, "afford all those interested an opportunity to view and to study the conditions surrounding . . . early American home life."[2]

To cull a handful of masterworks from such extraordinary resources offers a daunting challenge. Questions abound. Who should make the selection? What criteria should be used in the process? What weight should each criterion carry? What impression should be conveyed? Such basic questions trigger more practical concerns. Should the choices be based principally on beauty—an ambiguous term that reflects personal perceptions of artistic achievement? Or should economic value—either now or at the time of manufacture—influence the decision? Should the importance of an object to its original owner or subsequent owners, including du Pont, affect the selection process? Should the objects collectively present the entire chronological and stylistic sweep of the collection? Or should objects be segregated by medium and treated as benchmarks of a specific craft? Can each object stand alone as a masterwork in its own right or must it be seen within a broader cultural context? Such issues sparked considerable debate during the preparation of *Eye for Excellence*. The resulting decisions reflect a long-standing interest among Winterthur curators in the topics of connoisseurship and craftsmanship as well as a traditional division of decorative arts by material.

At Winterthur, curators specialize in specific media. A similar approach was adopted for *Eye for Excellence*. The categories of metalwork, glass, ceramics, furniture, textiles and embroidery, paintings and prints, and books and manuscripts became the framework for the project. Curators were given the task of choosing objects that they considered to be masterworks in their areas of expertise. Three criteria guided the selection process: exceptional artistic expression in concept and design, masterful manipulation of materials, and clearly defined cultural attributes. Although succinct and seemingly straightforward, these factors leave considerable room for interpretation. For example, while one curator may equate artistic expression with ambitious ornament, another may consider the stark simplicity of a graceful curving outline or a rational system of proportion as important components.

As the process of selection unfolded, various issues became key factors for individual curators. Robert Trent chose to emphasize recent breakthroughs in the conservation of painted furniture and new areas of collecting interest such as original upholstery. His objects differ dramatically—from the sculptural contours of a Native American bowl to the gilt flamboyance of a French-inspired neoclassical armchair. For Trent, furniture becomes an index of the rich, multifaceted mix of cultural influences in early America. Sherry Fowble sought specific paintings and prints as exemplars of artistic trends in America. Her choices extol the artist's ability to convey the vitality, philosophy, and spirit of a particular time and place. Deborah Kraak elected to juxtapose the unique embroidered achievements of schoolgirls with commercially printed textiles of exceptional quality. Although one form was individually produced for use or display in a particular home and the other was manufactured for wide distribution, the two often share a common design vocabulary. Curving floral branches, for example, decorate many of the best eighteenth-century textiles at Winterthur. Donald Fennimore approached the subject of metalware from a broad perspective, choosing to include seven different materials rather than concentrate on the traditional symbols of quality, silver and gold. His decisions spring from a deep-seated belief that artistic excellence may appear in any material regardless of price or use. Like Fennimore, Amanda Lange identified a broad range of objects within her specialties, glass and ceramics. Her selections chronicle the history of both media within America during the eighteenth and early nineteenth centuries. Like Kraak, she highlights rare presentation pieces as well as more ubiquitous forms that were made in sizable quantities. Finally, Neville Thompson's selections feature drawings and books that resulted from extraordinary efforts—true labors of love—on the part of their makers or publishers. Their dedication transformed such mundane exercises as scientific illustration into works of art.

The essays and entries that follow reveal the stunning quality of the Winterthur collection to be sure. But they also reveal the individual perspectives of the curators. Each has adjusted the criteria of selection slightly; each has charted a singular course in presenting the selections in this catalogue. Their approaches affirm the individuality of artistic appreciation, for, indeed, everyone looks at objects differently. Deciding what is best from a particular group is a highly personal process for each and every one of us. There are no right or wrong answers, only questions to be asked of an object and opinions to be formed. No two items, for example, could appear more disparate than John Singleton Copley's sophisticated self-portrait and Forbes Clark's mammoth copper fish kettle. Yet these two objects represent the pinnacle of their respective crafts in early America. They communicate something about the artist and craftsman and about the time and place in which they were made. They also celebrate the technical expertise and skillful eye of the maker as well as the discerning eye of the collector and curator. In doing so, they, and all the selections that follow, epitomize the meaning of masterwork.

Brock W. Jobe
Deputy Director
Collections and Interpretation

[1] John A. H. Sweeney, *The Treasure House of Early American Rooms* (New York and London: W. W. Norton, n.d.); Arthur J. Sussel to H. F. du Pont, December 18, 1931, box 57, Winterthur Archives; quoted in Jay E. Cantor, *Winterthur* (New York: Harry N. Abrams, 1985), p. 179.

[2] Charles F. Montgomery, "Thoughts upon the Twentieth Anniversary of the Winterthur Program," April 5, 1974, H. F. du Pont biography material, Winterthur Archives.

METALWORK

Quality is an abstract concept and as such is difficult to define. It describes the way we perceive our environment, both individually and collectively. In essence the word is meaningful only in a comparative context, that is, in identifying a degree of excellence in something when contrasting it with others of the same kind. Simply stated, it is something that we all seek, whether it be in circumstances, relationships, or material surroundings. The purpose of this essay is to explore my perception of quality with respect to the last of these—material objects.

From a logical vantage, the concept might be seen as nonsensical. If, for instance, two teapots are equally capable of containing and accurately dispensing their contents into a teacup, of what real significance can their relative quality be? Some would argue that one is as good as the other, that constructing a hierarchy in which one is ranked as having greater quality than the other is not only irrelevant but a wasteful use of mental energy. Logic would seem to support such a contention. Yet, humans are not exclusively logical beings. There is an element in our psyche that prevents us from being completely dispassionate. We interact with our surroundings both physically and emotionally. That emotional component can and often does have far-reaching consequences that govern the matter of quality in objects. Our physical involvement with objects can be measured in the present—grasping a teapot's handle, picking it up, directing it over a teacup, and tilting it forward at the correct angle to pour its contents. Emotional involvement can also be measured in the present—the capacity of the teapot's shape, texture, and materials (separate and apart from its contents) to attract our attention and make us want to reach out for it—as well as the future—as with any sense of satisfaction or dissatisfaction generated by the teapot. If we were to respond positively, we would probably conclude that "this is good. I will live with this teapot, and if I ever have to replace it, I will do so with another just the same." If we were to respond negatively, we might well conclude that "it could be better." With that observation follows the decision to design, make, or more likely, purchase another that is more satisfying. Either response determines the course of evolution in teapot shape, texture, and materials. That both are possible indicates the fluid nature of ascribing quality to an object and, very importantly, the subjective or personal forces at work in doing so.

Another important factor implicit in the statements "this is good" and "it could be better" is that the individuals making them believe they are fully qualified to recognize and make judgments about quality. Rarely will anyone faced with the opportunity of making a statement about the goodness or badness of something refrain from doing so. Opinion with respect to quality is rampant and often stated with conviction.

Some who offer opinions on quality in artifacts, when pressed to elucidate, couch their pronouncements in such euphemisms as "it just is" or "if you don't know, I can't explain it to you." Such statements imply that a human hierarchy exists containing two types of people: those who are born with an ability to see and make judgments about matters of quality and those who are not—and there is no bridge between the two. This contention is not necessarily to be condemned if, for the individual expressing the opinion, determining relative merit in an object is a solitary endeavor, without the sharing of opinion or exchanging of views. Such individuals serve as their own index to the environment. If, on the other hand, perceptions of quality are acknowledged to be societal phenomena, wherein a community of individuals explores, develops, refines, and builds a framework with which to make judgments about objects, then any statement regarding quality must be supported by a rationale. Otherwise, no accurate sense of an opinion can be conveyed.

This essay is built around metal objects chosen to present a broad spectrum of media and working techniques. I maintain that they are of paramount quality in an early American (1640–1860) context. Everyone who looks at them may readily agree, their materials and configuration being such that my assertion will be deemed obvious. Were this a likelihood, we would need only to observe, enjoy, and reflect in silence. Human nature being what it is, however, I will more likely be met with agreement by some, disagreement by others, and a quizzical scratching of the head by still others. I, therefore, must attempt to justify my position.

All metals possess certain physical properties, including ductility, malleability, hardness, tensile strength, fusibility, color, and inertness. These properties vary from one metal to another and suit each to a unique range of uses. Although iron's hardness makes it appropriate for use in door locks, it quickly corrodes, making it unsuitable for water containers. Gold's inertness renders it excellent in contact with acidic human skin, but its softness means it will not withstand use as a kitchen spatula. From a practical vantage then, no metal has greater quality than any other. Each, with its particular combination of physical properties, fills a specific niche in the spectrum of human needs.

Despite this objective approach, the concept of quality has been incorporated into the realm of metals and is typically indexed to something very subjective, which I call significant assigned value. Within the parameters of Winterthur's collections significant assigned value equates with gold and silver. Since time out of mind, gold and silver have symbolized quality, due in part to an emphasis on two of their physical properties—color and inertness—and to their relative rarity. So ingrained is the equation of these metals with the idea of quality that it is not a matter for conscious thought. It just is, and although the base metals iron, copper, zinc, tin, and nickel have served mankind in many important ways for millennia, never have they been assigned an equal level of quality based on material.

Related to this concept of significant assigned value are several other observations that can be made with respect to perceptions of quality in metal. One involves weight. Metals, whether in a raw state or in the form of finished goods, have traditionally been sold by weight. The greater the weight, the greater the cost. Simple economics governs the principle; this has led to a popular perception that equates weight, cost, and quality. The greater the weight, the greater the cost, and the greater the cost, the greater must be the quality.

Closely aligned with this equation is the matter of size, which people often use to help determine their response to an object. This practice is well understood and accepted in the examination of objects as diverse as diamonds and buildings, and it applies equally to metals. Brass andirons or silver candlesticks, for instance, if of large or larger-than-normal size, have a greater capacity to impress than their smaller counterparts. This capacity is often expressed in terms of quality.

Still another factor that can color our perception of quality in an object is its intended purpose. Our lives revolve around an elaborate and complicated mix of custom and ritual. Objects play important and often central roles in many of these activities. Some objects are used in ceremonies that demand deference on the part of the individuals interacting with them, as with a pewter chalice on an altar. Others, like pewter commodes, unarguably fulfill equally important functions, from both a practical and social perspective, but at a level that engenders no sense of admiration. The former objects, by virtue of their exalted roles, are often associated with the concept of quality, whereas the latter are not.

Quantity of ornament always seems to have been inextricably linked to quality. With few exceptions, ornament on metalwork, whether cast, chased, engraved, inlaid, applied, or colored, is added separately and apart from fabrication. The processes involve labor, which of necessity generates additional cost. The more ornament added, the greater will be the final cost of the object. Since cost has always been associated with quality, it follows in the minds of many that the greater the quantity of ornament added to an object, the better its quality will be.

The five factors discussed here—material, weight, size, function, and quantity of ornament—*can* contribute to an object's quality. If they were the sole determinants, however, any large, heavy, elaborately decorated, gold ceremonial vessel would, by definition, be of excellent quality. Conversely, any small, lightweight, plain, iron utilitarian object would be wanting in quality. This, of course, is not the case. Each of the aforementioned factors is important but not central to determining quality in metalwork. I believe the answer lies elsewhere.

If a single word were chosen to represent the answer, I believe it would be *beauty*. Admittedly, beauty means many things to many people. It represents a complicated, subjective interaction between individual and object but, nonetheless, seems to be the one word that springs to mind most readily to identify and capture the essence of quality in an object. It is an oft-used word, but one that I believe is cited with little sense of definition.

For me, beauty in an object is the capacity to please. More specifically, it is the ability of an object to satisfy visually and stimulate intellectually. An object is no more capable of acquiring those attributes on its own than it is of making itself. An artisan (artist, craftsman) imbues an object with beauty; by analyzing the creative input, we can derive insight into what makes an object beautiful. In creating an artifact, an artisan exercises two talents that are enlightening for us, one is technical and the other artistic.

Technical proficiency is an acquired talent, achieved through practice and training. Any artisan can expect to reach the level of ability at which manipulating materials with dexterity is achieved, but some will exceed that level and develop so good an understanding of the material's working properties that they can manipulate it at will, virtually as second nature. In addition, some artisans achieve the rarified ability to not just manipulate but manipulate masterfully. With that mastery, an artisan can achieve any desired effect, whether it be blue or white, smooth or rough, delicate or massive, flowing or immovable.

Artistry, on the other hand, is an inborn talent and, in my opinion, is most difficult to identify tangibly. Artisans who lack it merely make objects. Those fortunate enough to possess it have the ability to conceptualize an object before it exists. They make objects that serve but also inspire. With artistry, an artisan can imbue an object with spirit, which might be thought of as the essence of an idea. Art historians describe that sense of an idea through the concept of style—Gothic, mannerist, rococo—but for artisans gifted with this native ability, style is only part of it. For them, artistry is understanding an object in the context of its purpose so that a clear sense of function is conveyed and use is easy. It is, however, also much more. Artistry is a way of seeing that understands proportion—an object's mass or the relationships among its components—and allows creation of a logical whole. It is the ability to create a profile, surface, or ornamental motif that has its own dynamic identity. At the same time, it is the ability to integrate profiles, surfaces, and ornamental motifs in such a way that they complement and contrast with one another to create a satisfying whole. By integrating use (function) and appearance (nonfunction) into a visually satisfying whole, the gifted artisan creates, not just makes, an intellectually stimulating artifact. For me, this is the essence of what makes quality in metalwork.

Objects that possess this essence transcend time in the sense that they are free from the vagaries of ever-changing fashion. They, like a Michelangelo sculpture or a Rembrandt painting, are always looked upon as worthy of admiration. They are capable of stimulating inquiry into abstruse concepts such as what makes beauty or even why man alone has a need to practice its creation. Once created, these objects are literally capable of affecting, even altering, how individuals perceive their environment.

Among the most superlative expressions of quality in metalwork for me are the exquisitely conceived silver tureens created by Juste-Aurèle Meissonier for the Duke of Kingston in 1734 and the beguilingly attractive Barcelona chair designed by Ludwig Mies van der Rohe for the German pavilion at the International Exposition of 1929 in Barcelona, Spain. Within a functional context the former is pure ornament, whereas the latter is pure form; yet both strike the senses forcibly and in the same way—with an overpowering sense of correctness and timeless beauty. I do not suggest that the metal objects included herein should be viewed against the world class *chef d'oeuvres* of Meissonier and van der Rohe but within an American context. They are, undoubtedly, paramount expressions of technical mastery combined with gifted artistry. Their creators are among the few who acquired consummate control over their material while applying superb artistic sensibilities. It is those few who have set the rules that govern what makes objects beautiful. It is they who have created the artifacts included in the metalwork section of this catalogue.

Coffeepot, 1740–58
Jacob Hurd (1702–58), Boston
Silver, wood; H. 9⅞", W. 8⅝", Diam. 5¼"
60.1048 Gift of H. F. du Pont

Silver, like wrought iron, is exceptionally responsive to manipulation by a talented artisan. Its plastic nature allows it to be fashioned into an infinite number of shapes. This pliant characteristic encourages experimentation and elaboration, which renders the apparent simplicity of this coffeepot all the more striking. Its stately, truncated conical shape is gracefully proportioned, the pronounced taper adding to its sense of height. The shape is crisp and punctuated with discreet amounts of chaste ornament, the maker having resolutely resisted the temptation to blur the outline with an overload of detail. The broad expanse of brilliant, unblemished reflective surface, unforgiving of any mistakes, bespeaks a maker confident in his technical abilities and aesthetic sensibilities. It also serves as the perfect foil for the exquisite jewel-like engraving that forms the visual and conceptual focal point of this creation.

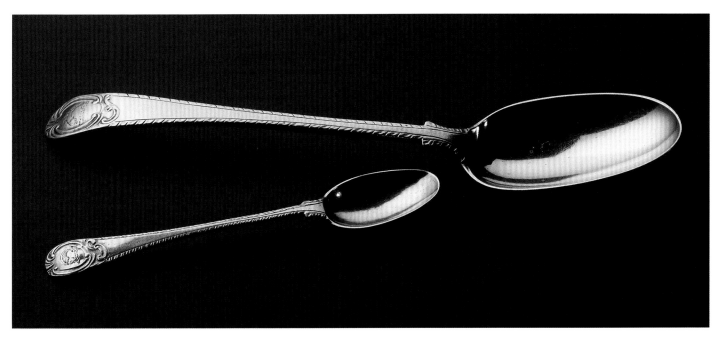

◀ Pair of candlesticks, 1760–80
Probably Canton, China, possibly England
Paktong; H. 12¼", W. 5⅝", D. 5⅝"
56.22.2, 56.22.3

When Leonardo da Vinci drew his concept of perfect proportion, he used a man, his arms and legs outstretched, within a circle and a square. His approach was simplicity itself, making the human figure the index for two of the most basic shapes in the built environment. The resulting design is visually satisfying and intellectually stimulating.

The same observation can be made about these candlesticks. The eye and mind step, as if on the rungs of a ladder, from square to circular shape, five times. Within the framework of this formula, the maker has heightened appeal by avoiding predictable regularity. He has varied size and detail, being careful to delineate and proportion each design element so it can be easily encompassed. At the very center we meet with an unexpected surprise, multiple piercing that allows light—and sight—to pass through what in most candlesticks is a solid shaft.

▲ Teaspoon and tablespoon, ca. 1781
Paul Revere (1735–1818), Boston
Silver; (teaspoon) L. 5⅜", W. ¹⁵⁄₁₆", D. ⅜";
(tablespoon) L. 9", W. 1¹¹⁄₁₆", D. 1¹⁄₁₆"
62.240.561, 62.240.1403
Gift of Mr. and Mrs. Alfred E. Bissell

Spoons have had a constant presence on American dining tables and have changed little since the early eighteenth century. Consequently, we pay them scant attention and rarely think of them as significant artistic statements. Yet, like any artifact, they can be an expressive medium for the creative mind.

These matching spoons are a classic example. Their straightforward purpose masks a richness of design and technical virtuosity that can be enjoyed casually but understood only with critical scrutiny. Far from being flat, these spoons are strongly sculptural, with downswept handle ends moving against compound upwardly curved bowls that impart a sense of dynamic but balanced tension. The quality of undulating movement along their lengths is subtly infused with torsional energy by the asymmetric C-and S-scrolls on both front and back, an exceptionally rare feature in American rococo flat silver. The result is eminently satisfying to the eye and in the hand.

21

Chimneyback, 1766–74(?)
Aetna Furnace (1766–74[?])
Burlington County, N.J.
Cast iron; H. 31½", W. 30", D. 1¹⁄₁₆"
58.2750

I look on this chimneyback with no less admiration than that for the tympanum of a superlative Philadelphia high chest. Had the object been a blank square, it would have worked just as well. Its maker envisioned something more, however. This tabula rasa was an opportunity to create a focal point of interest in what otherwise would be a black hole. The maker did so by adeptly shaping the top edge as a series of graduated opposing arcs that build to a crescendo, drawing the eye upward toward the center. Below, the animated figure of a gracefully modeled prancing stag loosely framed by naturalistic motifs does the same. The maker then added significantly to the sense of lightness and grace of this composition by placing the stag on a kinetically charged spring in the form of leafy scrolls. The result is not only visually pleasing but also temperamentally uplifting. This chimneyback is a supremely successful resolution to a difficult design challenge in a medium that does not often encourage artistry.

Fish kettle, 1807–35
Forbes Clark (1779–1835), Harrisburg, Pa.
Copper, iron; H. 17", W. 13⅛", L. 24¼"
90.51 Partial funds for purchase
gift of Eddy Nicholson

Those accustomed to thinking of quality in association with precious metals and ceremonial purpose will readily dismiss this copper and iron fish kettle. I believe that would be a mistake. Although made of relatively inexpensive metals and intended to serve a humble purpose, this vessel was fashioned by a craftsman who was sensitive to good design. That, coupled with the workmanlike construction and finish, makes this a creation of excellent quality. The most telling factor in support of this contention is proportion. The kettle's maker could have fashioned it longer, narrower, shallower, deeper, or with square corners, all of which would have significantly altered its appearance. The ratio of height to width to length—enhanced by gently flaring ends and a graceful arc that scribes the contour of the walls, the arch of the base, and dome of the removable lid—has been calculated to transcend mere utility. The result is an object subtlely infused with lightness and elegance that impresses the viewer as comfortably pleasing.

Chandelier, 1850–60 ▶
Attributed to Henry N. Hooper
and Company (1832–68), Boston
Brass, iron, glass; H. 50", Diam. 34"
91.41

Complex yet scintillating and vibrant describes
my reaction to this fifteen-light gas-candle
chandelier. Produced during an age when
complexity and elaboration were admired in
everything from literature and table manners to
architecture and fashion, this parlor fixture
embraces those concepts with abandon. Its
convoluted tendrils and lush genus-specific
flowers writhe with nervous energy. Points of
reflected light emanating from burnished areas
set amid a matted ground tease the eye
and challenge the mind to a constant state
of animation.

The anonymous designer clearly had an
affinity for French rococo design of a century
earlier. Yet, the French genre was not slavishly
copied. Instead of reiterating generic
compositions of C-scrolls, acanthus leaves, and
falling water, the designer adapted that aesthetic
by using flowers, buds, and entwined tendriled
vines. The effect is a familiar yet fresh
interpretation that stands as an icon of its era.

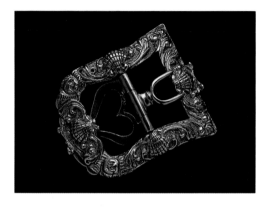

▲ Knee buckle, 1750–80
Philip Syng, Jr. (1703–89), Philadelphia
Gold; L. 1⅝", W. 1¼", D. ¼"
68.304 Gift of Lammot du Pont Copeland

Humans need to express themselves.
Language, body language, and dress are
among our most favored techniques. Each
conveys a person's character and self-
perception to others. In the area of dress,
jewelry can be one of the most expressive
means to communicate attractiveness, taste,
wealth, and even uniqueness.

This knee buckle—originally one of a
pair—although small, is a powerful statement
of its original owner's identity. It was made
entirely of the most precious metal then
known, gold. That alone was not enough for
its owner, however, who had its entire
presentation surface elaborately worked in a
florid composition of four scallop shells
flanked by leafy boughs, alternating with two
human masks and two floral sprays, all
against a pebbled ground. It is rich in
material, workmanship, and design. As such,
the buckle is a dynamic and evocative
expression of personal wealth and taste.

Flagon, 1766–87
Philip Will (1738–87), New York City
Pewter; H. 13", W. 7¾", Diam. 5½"
82.5

The Eucharist, or sacrament of the Lord's Supper, is one of the most sacred rituals in Christian culture. Those who participate do so with a sober and pious attitude; the ceremony is meant to impress its participants with the power and grace of God. Accordingly, any artifact associated with the sacrament should be designed so that it tangibly conveys these values. It should be grand, stately, imbued with a sense of eternity, and should also clearly transmit Christian concepts of beauty and love.

Designed and made in accordance with these values, this flagon is a simple and graceful towerlike structure that suggests clarity of purpose. Its verticality is organized into pleasingly proportioned units by horizontal moldings at the base and midsection. The same design element has been expanded to shape the domed lid. The sweeping contours of the handle enhance the flagon's height, while its conforming moldings and spurs at the juncture of the opposing curves complement and reinforce the importance of the moldings encircling the body. This flagon is a timeless document of the Christian ethic.

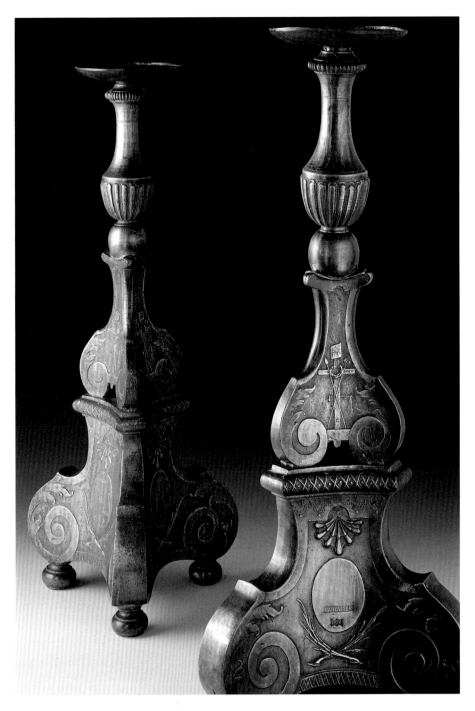

Pair of candlesticks, 1752–81
Marked by Johann Christophe Heyne
(1715–81), Lancaster, Pa.
Pewter, tinned sheet iron
H. 21⅞", W. 7¾", D. 8⅝"
65.1602.1, 65.1602.2 Gift of H. F. du Pont

These candlesticks, from a set of six, originally
graced the altar of the Church of the Most
Blessed Sacrament in Goschenhoppen, Berks
County, Pennsylvania. Although tall altar
candlesticks of similar design in silver, pewter,

and gilt wood were common in eighteenth-
century Europe, these having an American
context are unique.

The architecturally inspired graduated
baroque scrolls are grandly conceived and
boldly executed. The sweeping contours
dramatically frame ancient and very
recognizable Christian iconography, most
notably Christ's monogram and the symbols
of His Passion: the cross, hammer, scourge,
crown of thorns, spear, and vinegar-soaked

sponge. The candlesticks rise to imposing
height through slender balusters and widely
dished bobeches. The balusters are encircled
with alternating convex and concave
gadroons that, in concert with other motifs
raised above the surface of the candlesticks,
cast striking shadows and create highlights.
The towering and palpable presence
represents the Roman Catholic tradition in
eighteenth-century America at its richest.

EMBROIDERY
PAINTINGS
AND PRINTS
BOOKS AND
MANUSCRIPTS
METALWORK

GLASS

AMANDA E. LANGE

Given its fragile and impermanent nature, glass has always been an intriguing and mysterious material—easy to destroy and very difficult to mend. Melting common ingredients together such as sand and ashes produces a material that can be transformed into innumerable shapes, colors, and textures. When molten, glass has the properties of plasticity, fluidity, and ductility. When cooled, it forms a hard, noncrystalline substance that is sometimes transparent. It is almost impossible to imagine daily life without glass, yet we often take it for granted.

Winterthur collects glass that was made or used in America from 1640 to 1860. From this group I have selected objects that I believe illustrate the qualities of a masterwork. Each displays excellence in one or more of the critical areas of overall form and proportion, quality of workmanship, technical achievement, and aesthetic impact (which includes the features of color, light refraction, and decoration). For me, all of these factors are crucial components of a masterpiece in glass. Too often we are dulled to the beauty of glass by the large amount of it that fills our lives. To most of us, it is ordinary and rarely reaches the level of interesting. I have carefully studied and selected these few objects to bring to light the skill and ability of glass artisans.

Like other craftsmen, glassmakers need to understand their material, the methods of working and manipulating it, and its strengths and limitations. Years of apprenticeship and dedication to the craft tradition enable a glassblower to create competent objects. Those seen here display not only that rudimentary knowledge of the medium but also a confidence, control, and exuberance. Each demonstrates how glass has been manipulated to create not only a useful object but also an artwork of supreme beauty, creativity, and originality.

Discovered more than 5,000 years ago, glass developed out of experiments with colored glazes on ceramics. Glass has historically had varying economic value depending on the type of object, intricacy of decoration, and available technology. The earliest glass objects were small beads, seals, and inlays. Vessels of glass began to be produced around 1500 B.C. in Mesopotamia and later in Egypt. Glass objects were either cast in molds or wound around a core of clay and organic material. Because of the skill and labor involved, glass was a rare luxury in ancient Mesopotamia and Egypt and could only be afforded by the wealthy; glass vessels used for perfume and cosmetics were deposited within the tombs of the aristocracy for the afterlife. Until the first century B.C. glass was treasured like gold or precious gems.

With the invention of the blowpipe around 50 B.C. in the eastern Mediterranean, glass could easily be formed into unlimited shapes, sizes, and thicknesses. This hollow metal tool saved enormous amounts of time and labor and is the most important technological development in glassmaking. The introduction of full-sized, multipart molds also made replicating and decorating glass objects very efficient. During the first centuries of this era, glassmaking spread throughout the Roman Empire, and objects made of glass became increasingly available. After the fall of Rome, glassmaking declined in Western Europe. It was not until the early nineteenth century that the craft again reached a similar level of mass production and affordability. Of the millions of glass objects produced in the seventeenth, eighteenth, and nineteenth centuries, only a handful have survived intact. As a result, these objects have assumed a value (both aesthetic and monetary) unrelated to their original supply.

The rise of the English glass industry began in 1676 with the perfection of a glass resembling rock crystal, also known as lead glass. Experiments and innovations by George Ravenscroft (1632–83) led to the development of this new type of glass, which incorporated lead oxide into the formula. Lead glass is heavy, soft, and spectacularly brilliant, and it eventually became the standard in England and the envy of Europe. As the English glass industry flourished, the properties of lead glass were adapted to new designs, which were perfected in the eighteenth century. Perhaps the most magnificent, artistic property of lead glass is its power of light refraction, which imparts its brilliance. As light rays pass through the glass they are bent to form a prism of colors. The high refractive index is enhanced when the material is cut and polished, making it a natural for use in lighting devices such as chandeliers.

In the seventeenth century chandeliers were made of various materials, such as carved wood, silver, brass, and bronze, and they were sometimes hung with drops of rock crystal to increase the reflection of light. Later in the century the French began adding drops, or *pendeloques*, of glass from the candle arms.[1] Chandeliers composed entirely of glass began to be produced in England and Europe in the early 1700s, with the first advertisement for an all-glass chandelier in England appearing by 1714. By using cut lead glass, the light produced would have sparkled more brilliantly than with any metal chandeliers.

In the eighteenth century centerpieces made of glass were a dramatic focal point of the elite dessert table, where the elaborate and precise presentation of desserts was of primary importance. Delicacies such as fruits, cakes, and sweetmeats were often artfully stylized in the shape of a pyramid for decorative displays. Appearing in the late 1600s in England and around 1730 in

America, graduated glass salvers were placed one on top of the other, and jelly glasses were used to hold wet desserts.[2] An alternative to the glass pyramid was the sweetmeat pole. This structure is composed of a central spire with a top glass for an exotic fruit and attached arms with baskets for dry sweetmeats. A rare alternative to the sweetmeat pole and the stacked salvers was a combination of the two. Elaborate forms and intricate cut decoration made these dessert pyramids spectacular and awe-inspiring creations.

Although glassmaking was America's first industry (the earliest American glasshouse was established at Jamestown in 1608), few colonists operated successful glasshouses even in the eighteenth century. England prevented many skilled workers, including glassblowers, from leaving the country; often American glasshouses were staffed by immigrant German glassblowers. Eighteenth-century glass manufacturers met with fierce competition from foreign imports and with recurrent financial problems associated with massive operating costs. One such manufacturer was John Frederick Amelung, a German glassblower who arrived in Maryland in 1784. Settling in Frederick County, Amelung founded the New Bremen Glassmanufactory and produced the staples of every glasshouse, bottles and window glass, using green glass. His factory also created extraordinary refined, colorless tablewares, some of which were engraved for presentation. Amelung's workers showed a masterful manipulation of hot glass, exemplifying what a glassblower could do with the molten material and a variety of tools. Like those of many immigrant craftsmen, Amelung's products retained the styles and characteristics of glass made in his native region of Germany. He made sugar bowls with elaborate finials, covered tumblers, covered goblets, cream pitchers, salt dishes, pocket bottles, and case bottles. Strong competition from foreign glassmakers and a series of financial losses eventually drove him out of business.

As settlers moved west of the Allegheny Mountains, bottle glasshouses were established in western Pennsylvania, western Virginia, Ohio, and Kentucky in the early 1800s. In addition to producing bottle glass, these businesses also manufactured inexpensive tablewares. These so-called midwestern tablewares are known for their brilliant colors (amber, amethyst, olive, and blue) and pattern-molded shapes.

Color, or lack thereof, is one of the most important qualities of a glass object. The natural color of glass can vary from light green to dark olive, depending on the amount of iron impurities in the sand. The addition of mineral oxides (usually cobalt oxide for blue, gold or copper for red, and manganese dioxide for colorless or purple) to the mixture results in an assortment of colors. Glassmakers had varying success with their colorless glass and continually strove to create a glass recipe free of tint.

After the War of Independence, American merchants were finally able to trade freely with Continental sources. Almost immediately Americans began purchasing large quantities of glass products from Germany and Bohemia, areas well known for their wheel-engraving tradition. The hardness of Bohemian potash glass made it particularly suitable for wheel engraving, a process that uses rotating copper wheels and an oily abrasive. Many glass objects produced in

Bohemia were specifically designed to appeal to American sentiments and tastes; the Bohemians excelled in creating decoration exactly replicating English and American prints.

The development of the mechanical press in America during the 1820s was the most significant technological innovation in glassmaking since the invention of the blowpipe. The effects of this new technology were profound: production soared, prices fell, and new markets opened. Mass production became a reality; hot glass could be pressed against the surface of a metal mold, creating form and decoration at the same time. Artistry and skill shifted from the glassblower to the moldmaker. Intricate floral and geometric designs were used to obscure the cloudy surfaces and unattractive wrinkles associated with early pressed glass. Thousands of molded patterns were created to keep up with the growing demand for novel styles. Further advances in the technology reduced the cost of glass to the consumer, and glass became increasingly more common on American tables.

Although ubiquitous and ordinary in our daily lives, glass, when worked and ornamented in extraordinary ways, becomes an expression of true artistry. As can be seen in the objects I have chosen, simple molten sand and ashes are miraculously transformed into soaring and articulate masterworks.

---

[1] Ada Polak, *Glass: Its Makers and Its Public* (London: Weidenfeld and Nicolson, 1975), p. 143.

[2] Louise Conway Belden, *The Festive Tradition: Table Decoration and Desserts in America, 1650–1900* (New York and London: W. W. Norton, 1983), p. 55.

Chandelier, 1730–40
England
Lead glass; H. 47½", Diam. 47"
64.1009

English chandeliers are a feat of art and engineering. When candlelit, they create a dramatic and glittering display. Flickering candlelight is refracted and reflected in each faceted surface, magnifying the intrinsic brilliance of cut lead glass. This chandelier exemplifies the properties of lead glass and the skill of glass artisans. Its deeply curving, solid-glass candle arms almost swoop down upon you like the tentacles of an octopus. Although the elegant form appears striking and simple, the object is extremely complex and sophisticated. Its crucial structure is artistically hidden. A slotted metal plate, concealed in the silvered bowl, supports the full weight of the graceful arms. Broad, flat facets and decorative molding on the glass spheres obscure the supporting metal rod within. The result is a graceful and harmonious composition.

Before its purchase by Henry Francis du Pont, this chandelier hung on the ground floor grand hall of an English country house, Thornham Hall. It is one of the earliest surviving examples of early English glass chandeliers.[1]

---

[1] For more information see Arlene Palmer, *Glass in Early America: Selections from the Henry Francis du Pont Winterthur Museum* (Winterthur, Del.: Henry Francis du Pont Winterthur Museum, 1993), p. 324.

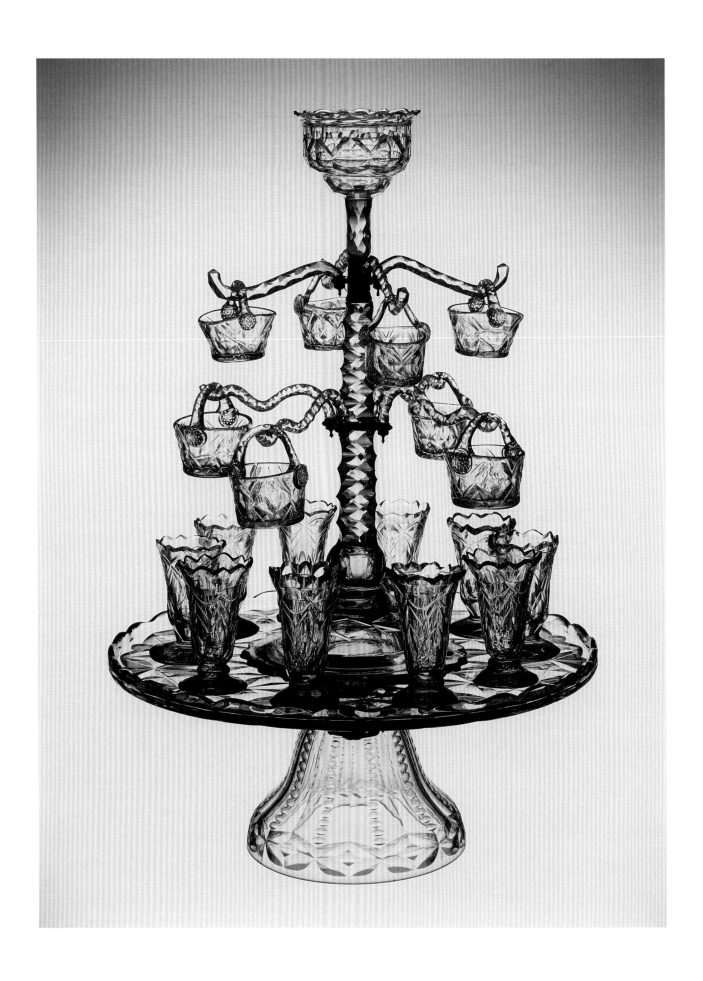

Dessert stand, 1765–75
England
Lead glass, silver; H. 23½", Diam. 15 %16"
Two baskets are modern replacements
90.86.1, 90.86.3–.12, 79.63a–r

This dessert stand would have been the sensational focal point of any dining table. Sugared sweetmeats filled the cut baskets, jelly glasses brimmed over with frothy confections, and other exotic fruit topped off the display. By candlelight, the sparkling brilliance and gleaming surfaces would be captivating. The glasscutter's knowledge and skill created an awe-inspiring composition of great beauty and drama. Excellent workmanship shows in the use of transparent lead glass rather than ceramic or metal and in the fabrication of the snakelike arms, solid glass pole, jelly glasses, and galleried stand and base. The glasscutter greatly enhanced the stand's beauty. Flat facets, V-shaped cuts, and diamonds give the object sharp, crisp surfaces, lightness and elegance of form, and an impression of fragility. We present the dessert stand as pictured in the circa 1769 advertising trade card of William Parker, a London glasscutter.

Photo courtesy Trustees of the British Museum

Sugar bowl, 1785–95
John Frederick Amelung's
New Bremen Glassmanufactory,
Frederick County, Md.
Nonlead glass
H. 8½", Diam. (top of bowl) 4⅜"
52.279a,b Gift of H. F. du Pont

This sugar bowl is the finest example of free-blown glass made at the New Bremen Glass-manufactory of John Frederick Amelung, and it is perhaps the most beautiful example of eighteenth-century American glass.[1] Amazingly, it has survived in perfect condition. For me, this sugar bowl gracefully and simply blends perfection of shape and design into one singularly beautiful object. By turning the hot glass at the end of a blowpipe and swiftly and surely using tools, the blower produced an artful composition. Neither strong color nor elaborate wheel engraving are necessary to enhance the elegant form. The swan finial is sheared and nipped to produce flared wings, a curved neck, and extended tail feathers.

[1] For more information, see Dwight P. Lanmon and Arlene M. Palmer, "John Frederick Amelung and His New Bremen Glassmanufactory," *Journal of Glass Studies* 18 (1976): 108–9.

Sugar bowl, 1820–45
Attributed to Zanesville, Ohio
Lead glass; H. 6 ", Diam. (top of bowl) 5"
59.3070a,b Gift of H. F. du Pont

Since ancient times, glassblowers have used glass to imitate precious materials, especially gemstones. This sugar bowl, with its rich blue color and diamond patterning, resembles a faceted sapphire. Often the color of glass is the most immediate and striking feature. When light interacts with a piece of colored glass, dark areas contrast with lighter ones for spectacular effects. The bowl's strong form enhances the brilliant color. Bold curves and small scallops compose its attractive profile. Collectors of early American glass prize this particular form of Ohio Valley glass tablewares. George McKearin, a glass dealer and scholar, said that he wanted a similar Zanesville sugar bowl buried with him.[1]

[1] Palmer, *Glass in Early America*, p. 209.

Vases, 1840–60
Bohemia
Nonlead glass, red stain; engraving: "BATTLE MONUMENT, BALTIMORE." and "THE PRESIDENTS HOUSE, WASHINGTON."; H. 13¾", Diam. 4⁷⁄₁₆"
92.119.1, 92.119.2 Partial funds for purchase gift of Mr. and Mrs. John R. Donnell

This pair of vases is a superlative example of Americo-Bohemian glassware, characterized by applied colored stain and wheel-engraved American images. These dramatic objects are enhanced by the contrast of surfaces: red stain, frosted engraving, and transparent cutting. Much more intricate than glass-cutting, wheel engraving demanded more skill and judgment on the part of the artisan. Engravers were able to reproduce images from American and English print sources with amazing accuracy. The scenes are rendered in minute detail, and the delicate rococo surrounds are fluid and graceful. These monumental vases once ornamented a tiered cabinet or mantelpiece of a lavish parlor of the mid nineteenth century. Their graceful, curving forms and bold, flaring rims would have impressed any visitor. In addition, their depiction of the two architectural icons of American democracy, the president's house (White House) and the Battle Monument of Baltimore, made them particularly appealing.[1]

---

[1]The engraving of the president's house in Washington is based on the print first published in 1831 by the English firm Fenner, Sears, and Company. The print source for the battle monument in Baltimore was a drawing by William Goodacre, an American landscape painter and drawing instructor. The print was published in 1831 by Archer and Boilly; see Jane Shadel Spillman, "Glasses with American Views," *Journal of Glass Studies* 19 (1977): 134–46; Jane Shadel Spillman, "Glasses with American Views, Addenda," *Journal of Glass Studies* 22 (1980): 78–81.

Compote (one of two), 1830–50
Massachusetts
Lead glass; H. 6¼", L. 10⁹⁄₁₆", W. 8⅞"
59.3068 Gift of H. F. du Pont

This striking yellow compote in the Princess Feather design is an early example of the revolutionary technology of glass pressing. Molten glass was squeezed into a metal mold so that form and decoration were produced simultaneously. The technique of pressing allowed glass objects to be made more quickly and cheaply but obviously did not eliminate quality. The early lacy patterns represent a design triumph over significant difficulties. The scrolls, shields, and acanthus leaves reflected light and obscured the inherent wrinkles and cloudiness that resulted from the pressing process.

CERAMICS

AMANDA E. LANGE

Pottery is among the most ancient of crafts. It reflects both the practical needs and the frivolous desires of a culture. The variety of ceramic objects is as extensive as the techniques used to form and decorate them. With such diversity, the selection of what I consider to be masterworks has been a challenge. A limiting factor, however, has simplified my task. The objects I have chosen represent the strengths of the Winterthur ceramics collection: Chinese export porcelain, English ceramics, and American pottery. They also all fulfill my criteria for a ceramic masterwork: technological skill, historical significance, quality of craftsmanship, and aesthetic appeal or impact. The final criterion of aesthetic appeal is the most difficult to define since it is so personal. For me, if an object has historic merit it ignites an emotional as well as an intellectual response.

Ceramics are tactile objects and demand to be experienced through touch as well as sight. Only then can the full achievement of the craftsman be understood, appreciated, and enjoyed. The earliest ceramic products were created more than 24,000 years ago. By 6400 B.C. potting had become a mature craft. Since then, the materials and processes have remained largely the same. Ceramics are fashioned from clay and other materials that are combined with water and are shaped, dried, and baked to form a rock-hard product. The most important property of clay is its plasticity, or the ability to be molded into a variety of shapes. Very often ceramics are coated with a layer of glaze, or glass, in order to seal the body and to decorate the surface.

Ceramic bodies such as earthenwares, stonewares, and porcelains are classified according to their clay components and relative baking, or "firing," temperatures in the kiln. Earthenwares are opaque, can be coarse in texture, and are fired at low temperatures. Because they are porous, they must be covered with a glaze in order to be impervious to liquids. Stonewares, which sometimes have a salt-glazed surface, are fired at a higher temperature than earthenwares; the clay becomes glasslike and impermeable to liquids. Porcelain bodies are usually white, hard, and translucent and are fired at the highest temperatures.

Since its perfection in China during the early part of the Tang dynasty (A.D. 618–906), porcelain has fascinated mankind. Chinese porcelain is usually composed of kaolin (china clay) and petuntse (china stone). The material was introduced into Europe in the sixteenth century, and Westerners went to tremendous lengths to possess it, to understand it, and to reproduce it. Porcelains of all kinds were regarded as special treasures to be ornamented in gilt-metal mounts and stored in cabinets. Chinese products reached Europe in limited amounts, and a great interest in all Asian exotic objects—porcelains, silks, lacquers—steadily grew among royalty and the wealthy upper class.

With the increasing fashion of tea, coffee, and chocolate drinking and the use of dinner services, the demand for and supply of Chinese porcelain increased dramatically in the early 1700s. The Chinese began making porcelain objects specifically for export to the West. The majority of this porcelain was based on European forms or prototypes. As early as 1635 the Dutch sent wooden models of contemporary Continental silver and pewter forms to China to be copied. They later sent ceramic, glass, and metal forms as models and popular prints to be depicted on the European shapes. The Dutch East India Company employed artists in the Netherlands to execute designs specifically for porcelain decoration. Perhaps the most intriguing facet of Chinese export porcelain is this integration of two vastly different cultures in one object.

Among the Western forms produced for export by the Chinese was the monteith. Monteiths, basins with notched rims, were used to cool wine bottles and decanters and chill and rinse drinking glasses. Glasses would hang by their feet along the notched rim. The earliest known monteiths date from the late 1600s, and they were most popular as a form in the early 1700s. Although the majority of monteiths were created in metal, a few examples occur in glass, tin-glazed earthenware, and Chinese export porcelain. Those created in porcelain represent a technical triumph for the potters. Because they are so large and intricate, they would have been difficult to fire without warping, slumping, or collapsing.

In addition to reproducing Western forms in porcelain, the Chinese also produced ornamented objects for export based on forms from their own culture, forms that would satisfy the European desire for the exotic. A favorite item, and the Chinese building type perhaps best known in Europe, was the pagoda. The popularity of this foreign architecture inspired many imitations, most notably William Chambers's Great Pagoda at Kew Gardens. Pagodas made of porcelain were often used for decorating hallways and alcoves of exotic rooms.

Americans finally began direct trade with the East when the *Empress of China* sailed from New York to Canton in 1784. We, like the Europeans, sent specific shapes and prints to be copied in porcelain, forms and scenes that would appeal directly to the American market. The reproduction of many of the Western prints in overglaze enamels is a tribute to the exceptional copying skill of the Chinese enamelers, especially since there was little or no communication between the artisans and their consumers.

The first successful white-bodied porcelain in Europe was produced in Florence, Italy, in the

1570s. This Medici body, however, was neither in composition nor in firing the true porcelain of China but was what is called artificial or soft-paste porcelain. The Meissen factory near Dresden, Germany, succeeded in making true porcelain by 1708, and by 1768 a few factories on the Continent and in England manufactured it with varying degrees of success. Most porcelain production in England in the 1700s focused on variants of the soft-paste porcelain recipe. The factories of Chelsea, Bow, Worcester, and Derby produced numerous utilitarian and decorative wares. Many of the figures they made are aesthetic and technical achievements in their masterful manipulation of the clay into different shapes and forms. A sweeping range in texture and forms was possible. The inspiration for porcelain figures was probably the confectionery sugar figures that the aristocracy and court had on their dessert tables. Figures made of porcelain were a permanent replacement for these fashionable items. In the 1700s figures were also used to ornament mantelpieces and display cabinets.

In the ninth century, an earthenware glaze was introduced into Western pottery from the Near East. It consisted of an aqueous lead glaze to which tin oxide was added for whiteness and opacity. The porous earthenware body absorbed the moisture of the glaze, leaving a white surface that was ideal for painted decoration. Tin-glazed earthenware was made all over Europe and was known as maiolica, faience, galleyware, bastard china, and delftware. The earliest evidence of the production of delftware in England is a record of a 1570 petition from Jasper Andries and Jacob Janson, two Flemish potters working in Norwich. The aesthetic quality of spontaneity is critical to the success of the product. The unfired glaze was chalky and porous, and a potter had to apply the decoration hastily and accurately. There was no room for error or erasures. Because the tin-oxide glaze imitated the whiteness of porcelain, many early English potters looked to Chinese porcelain for inspiration in decorating, often using the blue and white palette. In the mid to late seventeenth century, a thick pinkish white glaze with minimal decoration was also a popular style in delftware.

By the end of the 1600s, decorative ceramics were used on walls, dressers, and cabinets as a display of wealth. Bright, polychrome-painted delft dishes (erroneously called chargers) were sometimes covered with an exuberant tulip decoration, probably an influence from the Ottoman Empire. Tulips were introduced into Europe from Turkey in the sixteenth century, and in the seventeenth century these flowers inspired a passionate mania in Holland and England. In the eighteenth century delftware became the most common form of ceramic tableware in England and America.

With the rise of the commercial potting industry in the county of Staffordshire, England's role as an international center of ceramic production was assured. In the early 1700s, Staffordshire potters were among the first to respond to the new demand for fashionable tea and coffee wares. Potters moved away from the traditional coarse earthenwares to produce new types of refined earthenware and stoneware bodies. These were aimed at a growing middle-class market that could not afford to purchase costly Chinese porcelain. Josiah Wedgwood (1730–95), among others, helped Staffordshire potting to grow from a backwater, agrarian craft to an international industry. During his five years of partnership with Thomas Whieldon, his greatest achievement was the development of a new green glaze. Green glazes had been known earlier, but Wedgwood's exhibited a spectacular brilliance, especially when applied to creamware (cream-colored earthenware). The glaze was used on its own, in conjunction with other colors for apple and pear forms, and with a strong orange for pineapple and melon wares.

Red earthenware clay is perhaps one of the most humble and common materials known to man. It is found all over the world and is usually dug up along riverbeds; iron impurities color the clay a dark brown or red. Red earthenware production commenced very early in American history; as soon as colonists settled, potters began to make basic utilitarian storage, kitchen, and dairying wares. Many of these objects were plain, functional, and undecorated, and seventeenth-century American examples do not survive to any great extent. Highly decorated examples of American earthenware were usually made for ornamental purposes and have survived because they were special and valued.

Pennsylvania German sgraffito or scratch-decorated wares exuberantly display colorful decoration and energetic designs. A red earthenware body is covered with a layer of white slip (clay mixed with water); a potter then uses a stylus to scratch through the white slip to expose the red body below. Often sgraffito wares were additionally decorated with powdered metallic oxides and then lead glazed. The wares were often created to commemorate a special event and commonly were decorated with Germanic inscriptions. Sgraffito decoration can look surprisingly modern in its design and execution. Common motifs included galloping horsemen, vases of tulips, birds, leaping stags, and wavy-line borders, themes that belonged to several European regional traditions.

Sgraffito wares were first published and popularized in 1903 in Edwin AtLee Barber's *Tulip Ware of the Pennsylvania-German Potters*.[1] Soon after, the majority of existing wares were purchased by early collectors of American decorative arts. Sgraffito-decorated ceramics have a visual spontaneity and energy unequaled by other American ceramics. Their strong sense of movement, whimsy, and spirit capture the imagination. Because of the nature of the technique, it was not easy for the decorator to redraw a design or to correct mistakes. Many of the dishes show a bold draftsmanlike quality. Despite their impression of simplicity, these are well-designed objects.

The Shenandoah Valley, stretching from Chambersburg, Pennsylvania, to Harrisonburg, Virginia, is renowned for its rich ceramics heritage. The region has an abundance of workable, reddish-colored clays and a ready fuel source. The majority of the valley potters were either German immigrants or sons of immigrants. Working part of the year as farmers, they supplemented their livelihood by producing utilitarian ceramics for home and farm use. They also produced unique and special objects to commemorate important events and celebrate special occasions.

The Bell family was one of the most important and prominent potting dynasties of the area. Peter Bell, Jr., son of a German immigrant, established his first pottery in Elizabethtown (now Hagerstown), Maryland, in 1805. His oldest son, John, was one of the most successful Shenandoah Valley potters; he went on to have his own potteries in Chambersburg and Waynesboro, Pennsylvania. While Bell created numerous utilitarian wares, one of the most lively and novel objects he made was a figure of a standing lion. It is a powerful form that shows a degree of workmanship that is rarely encountered in American pottery. Bell combined a whimsical spirit with a mastery of his material.

Beauty, excellence, and mastery are all terms that are applied too easily. As you peruse this catalogue of masterworks, I hope that you will look first, read the entries second, and then challenge yourself to develop your own criteria for a ceramic masterpiece. I have provided some opinions and a path, but it is by no means the only one.

---

[1]Edwin AtLee Barber, *Tulip Ware of the Pennsylvania-German Potters: An Historical Sketch of the Art of Slip-Decoration in the United States* (Philadelphia: Patterson and White, 1903).

Monteith, 1720–30
China
Hard-paste porcelain with underglaze blue
and overglaze enamel decoration
H. 12⁵⁄₁₆", W. 17⅛", L. 20⅛"
60.763 Bequest of H. F. du Pont

The monumental size of this monteith would
have challenged the skill of any potter.[1] The
anonymous Chinese craftsman pushed the
limits of the porcelain clay almost to the brink
of collapse, wrapping large slabs around a
wooden form, smoothing and joining them
with liquid clay. By attempting to produce an
object this large and complex, he assumed the
significant risk of warpage and fractures
during firing. The result, however, is a highly
dramatic and arching shape. The crenelated
edge creates an intriguing variation of positive
and negative spaces. Small floral and geometric borders and clusters of foliage
and butterflies contrast sharply with the
whiteness of the porcelain body and the
strong geometric profile. The polychrome
coat of arms was added for an unidentified
European family.

---

[1] For more information about monteiths, see Jessie
McNab, "Monteiths: English, American, Continental,"
Antiques 82, no. 2 (August 1962): 156–60; Jessie McNab,
"The Legacy of a Fantastical Scot," *Bulletin of the
Metropolitan Museum of Art* 19, no. 6 (February 1961):
172–80; Edward Wenham, "The Bowl of Conviviality,"
Antiquarian 9, no. 6 (January 1929): 50–53.

Punch bowl, 1800–1810
China
Hard-paste porcelain with overglaze enamels
H. 6¼", Diam. 15⁹⁄₁₆"; inscription painted in
center of bowl in overglaze black enamel:
"SUCCESS TO THE SOUTHERN. HUNT." and in
overglaze orange enamel: "DW"
75.41

This Chinese export porcelain punch bowl is
decorated with a continuous scene of horses,
hunters, and hounds preparing for a fox hunt.
Tension and excitement are vividly captured.
The decorator of this bowl had superb
understanding of Western painterly techniques. The painter conveyed a sense of depth
and perspective, a purely Western concept.
Notice that the clouds are given shape and
definition by using a subtractive technique—
enamel was applied and then scraped off to
expose some of the porcelain body. Although
the scene was copied from a print source, the
decoration is not an enervated or slavish
reproduction but a dynamic reinterpretation
of an action-packed event.

Pagoda (one of two), 1785–1830
China
Hard-paste porcelain with underglaze
blue decoration; gilt wooden finials are
possibly later replacements
H. 60", W. 14¼"
59.3381a Bequest of H. F. du Pont

Tall and imposing, this pagoda dominates the
space around it. Imagine this exotic structure
placed dramatically in a hall or entryway. The
separately stacked roofs and stories are
perfectly proportioned to fit the ones above
and below. The intricacy of each railing, with
either opposing dragons or flower blossoms, is
remarkable. The underglaze cobalt blue
decoration articulates the whole structure in
an understated yet elegant manner. Western
merchants viewed pagodas when sailing to the
Chinese trading port of Canton. They were so
fascinated with the form that they imported
many decorative copies to Europe. The
majority were made of ivory, mother-of-pearl,
carved wood, soapstone, and jade. The most
impressive and beautiful pagodas were made
of porcelain; few were made in this
breathtaking scale.

Bottle, dated 1644
London
Tin-glazed earthenware with
enamel decoration; H. 6", W. 4¾"
64.684 Bequest of H. F. du Pont

This bottle demonstrates that excellence also
abides in humble objects and common forms.
Used for serving wine or spirits, the bottle has
the typical large belly, high neck, and
pronounced foot rim of the mid seventeenth
century. Its proportions are balanced, and its
curving lines are sinuous. The geometric
designs in cobalt blue enamel painted onto
the tin glaze are energetic, spontaneous, and
responsive to the form. Quick striking slashes
of a zebra-stripe pattern decorate the handle.
Geometric and stylized floral patterning on
the belly complement the globular roundness.
The potter was probably looking at Chinese
blue-and-white porcelain for his inspiration.
The color of the glaze, a mixture of creamy
white with a pinkish tinge, is also particularly compelling.

Cup, 1660–65
London
Tin-glazed earthenware with overglaze
enamel decoration; inscription in blue enamel
below rim: "CHARLES The 2D"
H. 2¹³⁄₁₆", W. 4⅝", Diam. 3⅛"
54.536 Bequest of H. F. du Pont

Ceramic cups have been made, used, and
discarded in vast numbers. Why did this one
survive? For one thing, it is a striking object.
The shape begs you to hold the cup and
coddle it. Its slightly bellied base, straight
sides, and circular handle are all perfectly
proportioned, deftly fulfilling their functions.
The opaque glaze exhibits subtle color
gradations of green, cream, and pink, which
appeal to the eye. The decoration shows an
economy of brushstrokes; a few swift dashes
of blue enamel outline and shade the figure.
The cup commemorates Charles II's restoration to the English throne in 1660.

Dish, 1670–90
London
Tin-glazed earthenware with overglaze
enamel decoration; H. 2⅜", Diam. 12⅛"
54.538

Decoration makes this dish extraordinary.
You can sense the quick, sure strokes of the
painter's brush in creating the superb design.
The exuberant motif conveys energy,
vitality, and confidence. London potters were
probably inspired by similar designs on
Turkish Iznik pottery. Paired blooms fill the
space and responsively curve to fit the slope
and profile of the dish. Diagonal blue dashes
around the rim attract your attention and
spiral your eye back into the composition.
The design is fresh and almost contemporary.
Such elaborately decorated dishes were
displayed on walls or in cabinets; they were
meant to be read like paintings. The foot
rim of this dish was pierced with a hole
for hanging.

Europe

America

Asia

Africa

The four continents or quarters, 1760–70
Attributed to Derby China Works
(ca. 1748–1848), Derby, England
Soft-paste porcelain with overglaze enamel
decoration, gilding
From left:
Europe: H. 12⅝", Diam. (base) 5⅜"
America: H. 12", Diam. (base) 5⅝"
Asia: H. 12¼", Diam. (base) 6"
Africa: H. 11¾", Diam. (base) 5⅜"
58.2622.2, 58.2622.3, 58.2622.1, 58.2622.4
Gift of H. F. du Pont

These figures display superior workmanship in their creation and execution. They represent four continents or the quarters of the globe: Europe, America, Asia, and Africa. Each continent is fashioned as a cherubic child with symbolic animals, flowers, and attributes of that specific land. These figures were manufactured as an assemblage of many complex, detailed molded parts. The modeling is masterful and intricate. Note the realism achieved in the camel's neck, Europe's drapery, and Africa's cornucopia. The skillful polychrome enameling balances color tones; no one color jars the group. Each figure combines the same turquoise, pink, and yellow enamels in different proportions, further uniting the set. Delicate brushstrokes carefully articulate the tiny hairs protruding from the elephant headdress, the bunch of grapes at the foot of Europe, and the floral designs on the silk gowns. Images of the four continents were popular and enduring in European decorative arts. The modeler at Derby may have had access to European porcelain versions created at the Meissen factory, but the ultimate source for the continents is Cesare Ripa's *Iconologia*, published in Rome in 1603, in which personified images of complex concepts such as the seasons, the elements, and the senses are depicted. A complete group of these large-sized figures in such good condition is a rare survival; only one other set is known to exist.

Tea and coffee wares, 1762–80
Staffordshire, England
Lead-glazed creamware with green glaze

Coffeepot: H. 10", Diam. 4⅛"
Milk jug: H. 6⁵⁄₁₆", Diam. 2⅜"
Waste bowl: H. 3⁵⁄₁₆", Diam. 5¹³⁄₁₆"
Plate: H. ⅞", Diam. 7¹¹⁄₁₆"
93.72a,b, 93.73a,b, 93.74, 93.85
Funds for purchase provided by the Collectors
Circle Fund, Mrs. W. L. Lyons Brown,
Mr. Charles O. Wood III,
and Mr. and Mrs. John A. Herdeg

Sugar bowl: H. 3¾", Diam. 4⁵⁄₁₆"
Cream pot: H. 3¼", Diam. 1⅝"
93.97a,b, 93.96 Funds for purchase provided
by the Friends of Winterthur

Tea canister: H. 5½", Diam. 3¾"
94.36a,b Gift of Edward J. and Mimi Nusrala

These green cauliflower wares demonstrate
a masterful accomplishment of Josiah
Wedgwood, whose name still connotes
well-made English ceramics. The brilliant, transparent green glaze was one of
Wedgwood's greatest achievements. Its
beauty and clarity, especially when applied to
creamware, was a stunning innovation in the
ancient technique of ceramic glazing. The
glaze articulates and energizes the leaves.
Where it pooled, the luscious coating
gives detail to the veining and depth to
the concavities.

These shapes were knock-offs, cheaper
imitations of fashionable porcelains produced
at the Longton Hall and Chelsea factories.
Wedgwood's moldmaker successfully imitated
nature and even improved upon it. My eye
delights in tracing the sinuous, writhing
motion of the green leaves and in gliding over
the nubby texture of the creamy white
vegetable. These objects possess a naturalistic
grace and vitality that have a timeless,
enduring appeal.

Plate, dated 1789
Attributed to George Hubener (1757–1828)
Upper Hanover Township, Montgomery
County, Pa.
Lead-glazed earthenware with white slip
and copper green oxide; inscription: "Susanna
Steltz; ihre schüssel; Alles was ihr wolt das
euch die Leute duhn sollen das duth ihr ihnen,
Merz. 5th 1789" (Susanna Steltz her dish. Do
unto others as you would have them do unto
you) and "Hir ist Abgebilt/ ein dabelter/
Adler" (Here is pictured a spread eagle)
H. 2¼", Diam. 13"
65.2301 Bequest of H. F. du Pont

This dish adorned with a double-headed eagle
and preening peacocks is a superior example
of Pennsylvania German sgraffito decoration.
Hubener's birds, flowers, and lettering are
boldly incised and perfectly laid out to fill the
limited space of the plate. The composition is
technically challenging. Curving lines join
and converge in graceful arcs as they integrate
Germanic lettering. The plate exhibits a
richness of texture and pattern, heightened
by the liberal use of green oxide. Sgraffito-
decorated ceramics were produced mainly
in a small area of southern Pennsylvania,
primarily Montgomery, Chester, and Bucks

counties. They are highly prized by American
ceramics collectors. This plate is one of
seventy-seven sgraffito objects that H. F.
du Pont purchased.

Dish, 1800–1820
Attributed to Johannes Neesz (1775–1867)
Tylersport, Upper Salford Township,
Montgomery County, Pa.
Lead-glazed earthenware with white slip and
copper green oxide; inscription: "Ich bin
geritten vihl stunt und Dag und Doch noch
kein metel haben mach" (I have been riding
night and day and no girl wants me anyway)
H. 1¾", Diam. 12¼"
60.619 Bequest of H. F. du Pont

Johannes Neesz was a farmer. Making redware storage jars, dairying wares, and kitchen crockery was a sideline business to supplement his income. With no formal training in design, his skill and facility with ceramic decoration is surprising. He produced many elaborate versions of this energetic horse-and-rider sgraffito design. His confident scratches into the white slip quickly give the impression of a horse in mid jump. The theme of the horse and rider was probably inspired by European examples depicting St. Martin or Frederick the Great; in Pennsylvania, the horseman design was reinterpreted to represent George Washington.[1] The entertaining and whimsical maxim provides an intriguing contrast with the noble image.

[1] Beatrice B. Garvan, *The Pennsylvania German Collection* (Philadelphia: Philadelphia Museum of Art, 1982), p. 165.

61

Dish, 1800–1825
Pennsylvania
Lead-glazed earthenware with white slip
and copper green oxide; H. 1⅞", Diam. 12⅛"
55.109.5 Gift of H. F. du Pont

This dish exhibits a compelling design,
showing the spontaneity and vigor of sgraffito
decoration, which is unmatched by other
American ceramics. The way in which the
curved forms of the three fish respond to one
another and to the rim of the dish is
particularly captivating. The extraordinary
simplicity and strong sense of line appeal to
contemporary tastes. I particularly like the
potter's creative use of a toothed tool to give a
sense of texture to the scales and fins of the
fish. Abstract swimming fish are an unusual
subject matter. The plate may have been used
to serve fish, or it may represent some implicit
Christian symbolism. The Greek initials for
Jesus Christ spell out the word *fish*, and the
fish is the oldest symbol for Christ.

Lion figure, 1840–65
John Bell (1800–1880), Waynesboro, Pa.
Lead-glazed earthenware with brown glaze
decoration; impression on rear leg:
"JOHN BELL"; H. 7⅜", L. 8½"
67.1630

John Bell hand modeled this novel and lively
lion. His success is not in realism or the
imitation of English prototypes but in the
originality, energy, and vitality of the figure.
Bell transformed the terrifying beast into a
gentle, smiling creature. The eye lingers over
the extruded clay mane, the toothy grin, and
the curling tail. Bell used brown glaze to give

a glossy, almost lustrous sheen to the mane
and the tail tuft. I find this object a pure
delight. It never fails to amuse me and to
exceed my expectations of what a ceramic
object should be. Researchers have con-
jectured that the lion functioned as a door
stop, but no one has proven this claim. The
rarity of such lions and their frequent
tradition of ownership by Bell descendants
support the contention that these figures were
made as special presentation gifts.

FURNITURE

ROBERT F. TRENT

It would be easy to list the numerous factors I consider when examining a piece of furniture—authenticity, context, function, structure versus ornament, concept versus execution, surface quality, and survival—as if they were a recipe for success: find the furniture, see if it meets the criteria, then declare it a masterwork! These factors are not a magic formula but the basic components needed to decide whether a piece of furniture is significant from both an aesthetic and historical point of view. Not all of the factors are necessarily objective, however. Insofar as artistic matters are concerned, the popularity of one style or another is not a matter of eternal truth but the result of modes of collecting. Styles that interest me the most are the mannerist style of the seventeenth century and the revival styles of the nineteenth century, although none of these has ever enjoyed the popularity of Queen Anne or Chippendale. Is this because Queen Anne and Chippendale are better? Certainly not, but people often assume so since these particular styles are collected by highly visible personalities.

Authenticity is paramount when determining the significance of furniture. An object that lacks a secure history of ownership rarely achieves the first rank of importance. Aesthetics cannot deliver the interpretive power of an exact origin. We value pre-1860 American furniture because we know it comes from a particular time and place. How the furniture reflects that context is a matter for debate, but first, to be worthy of the most profound inspection and introspection, the furniture must be genuine.

My next concern is establishing when furniture is art and when it is not. Artistic merit is not necessarily the key factor. A more objective standard might be that when someone with no knowledge of antiques feels that a piece of furniture is too old, too fragile, too beautiful, and too valuable to use, then it becomes art and "ought to be in a museum." This inarticulate need to preserve things in museums is central to our idea of art versus non-art.

Museum visitors expect to be told why furniture on view is significant. Some scholars believe furniture is meaningless outside an architectural context. Others might argue that the meaning of a given piece of furniture emerges only by comparison with like objects. Still others might ponder function—what the object was used for. Each of these ideas is stimulating, but each has problems.

The original architectural context of an object is rarely known. We may know what family it descended in, perhaps even the house it was originally used in, but not often can we point to the exact spot where the object stood or to what surrounded it. Without resorting to the use of reproductions alongside the real thing, we cannot recreate a completely accurate roomful of furniture. This is not to say that we cannot guess what a room might have looked like in the abstract.

In seeking like objects to compare to a given specimen, we may easily fall into mindless pigeonholing. The only people who might have thought about a category such as "all the chairs with pierced and carved slats made in this shop for the last six years" would have been the cabinetmakers. Customers would not have cared. So why do we want to line up all the objects in a given category? It is because we believe that sustained, systematic examination reveals both conscious and unconscious or habitual behavior that elucidates the creative process.

The question of function is a ticklish one. We can address technical functions (we sit on chairs, hence they must be made to sustain our weight) or ideological functions (this chair expresses allegiance to French style, hence French beliefs) or economic functions (only upper-class people can afford this chair). Function is all the more elusive because furniture is basically expressive *in intent*, which is not quite the same thing as function.

What is the distinction between structure and ornament, insofar as furniture is concerned? When cabinetmakers consider structure, they often concentrate on eliminating problems associated with objects made of wood, an intractable material. Occasionally they grapple with the stresses that are peculiar to seating or large bookcases. In any of these situations, structure rarely is considered apart from ornament. In the Gothic and Renaissance design traditions, ornament was implicit in most designs, not something added like frosting to a cake. Much of the expressiveness of furniture is communicated through ornament, an elaborate symbolic code that we absorb without clearly understanding it.

Another side of this analysis is the distinction between concept and execution. Each of us can visualize a chair of greater or lesser complexity, but few of us can make that chair. How does a vague idea become a finished product? One important intervening step is the working drawing. In it all extraneous detail is eliminated, and areas that are not well visualized must be pulled together. The parts must not only be drawn in detail but the joints for assembling them must be plotted. The materials must be selected with reference to the drawing. The surface regulation and treatment must be finalized. The contributions of other artisans like the gilder or the upholsterer must be indicated with exactitude. Nevertheless, a working drawing, no matter how detailed, no matter how enmired in pragmatic considerations, remains just a concept. The actual process of transferring the dimensions and detailing to the wood on the bench is part of execution. Note that I say execution, not workmanship. The terms *workmanship* and *artisanry* are too romantic to have exact meaning in modern discussions.

Perhaps the most evident way in which romantic notions hamper our thinking centers on surface treatments. We might make passing reference to color—in that Americans associate dark woods with formality and pale woods with informality—but the way in which the surfaces of furniture are treated is the most important key to an informed understanding of the medium. People believe workmanship may be inferred from surface qualities. If the surfaces of a piece of furniture are smooth and glossy, the joints are assumed to be conceived cleverly and made finely. If the surfaces are rough and lacking in luster, the joints are thought to be conceived with simplicity (if not naïveté) and executed with economy (if not crudity). But these widely held expectations do not always pan out. Many smooth, glossy veneered case pieces are poorly designed and shoddily constructed. Many rough, dull carpenter's workhorses are constructed with exacting specifications and precise joinery.

It is on the question of desirable surface qualities that the odd value system of modern collectors of American furniture is based. If the structure and ornament of a piece of furniture have survived reasonably intact (*how* they have survived never seems to enter into anyone's mind), then the surfaces must conform to certain abstract ideals that have no bearing on how the furniture looked originally. One hundred years ago the early collectors of American furniture refinished everything, perhaps because they associated crumbling finishes with the impoverished households from which much of the furniture emerged. Today collectors treasure old finishes—any old finish—for a variety of reasons. One, certainly, is fear of fakery, for cabinetmakers and painters have become adept at mimicking old finishes. It is only in the last decade that the chemistry and techniques needed to analyze furniture paints and finishes have been developed. We no longer need emote about such things; we can analyze them. Furthermore, we can responsibly and selectively clean finishes layer by layer until the point that irreversible alterations are being made to original material. Then, we stop.

I mentioned that it is difficult to reconstruct the original context for which a given piece of furniture was made. I also mentioned that little thought is given to how furniture survives. By European standards, American furniture is not old, unless you regard Native American objects as decorative arts, and then our date range expands considerably. On the East Coast the oldest furniture we know of dates from about 1635. To put this in some kind of perspective, only about twelve or thirteen generations separate us today from the settlers of the 1630s. If we have a note written in the 1850s by an eighty-year-old grandmother recording the line of descent for a chest owned by her ancestor in 1680, the elderly source is probably writing about her great-great-grandmother. Reading her note in 1994, we are close to the immediate circumstances under which the chest was made. But why was the history of the chest repeated? Indeed, why was the chest preserved? It may have had something to do with childhood memories of grandparents.

The manner in which something was preserved and the motivations of each generation that preserved it are central to interpretation. A museum is, after all, the last link in an extended trail of owners. Although we like to maintain the fiction that our furniture epitomizes the taste of its original owners, it in fact represents the taste of all its owners, including museum curators, or it would not have survived to be selected for purchase or gift to an institution in the twentieth century.

All the preceding commentary might seem like so much quibbling. Do I or do I not know a masterwork when I see one? And why did I choose the particular objects included here? As my selections might indicate, I am interested in presenting new accessions, new conservation achievements, and an extended date range for the collections. New accessions are represented by upholstered furniture, one of my fields of specialization. Some striking objects transformed by Winterthur's conservators, who have revolutionized the treatment of painted and gilded surfaces, can also be seen here. Finally, the entire chronological range of the museum's collections is represented. Although the choice of a Native American bowl might seem perverse, the object deserves to be interpreted as a masterwork and monument of ceremonial sculpture.

Looking at these objects, I hope the reader can appreciate the full panoply of factors I have raised. While I could have addressed these considerations with any number of pieces of furniture in the collection, those presented here are among the most meaningful and allow for an appreciation that encompasses the complexity underlying our attitudes toward them.

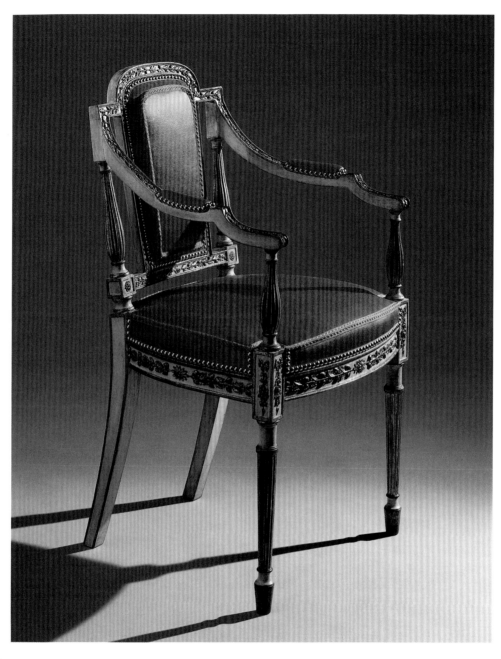

Gilt cabriole armchair, 1795–1805
Philadelphia
Ash; H. 36¼", W. 20½", D. 21⅝"
91.66

An anglicized version of a Louis XVI *fauteuil*, this armchair is executed in ash with composition ornament rather than in beech with carving partly in wood and partly in gesso, as was the practice in France. The frame retains the original stitched horsehair upholstery foundation with traces of the original orange silk covers. These fragile painted and gilded surfaces were very difficult to conserve, particularly because they had been overpainted with bronze pigment. The surfaces now visible represent a compromise presentation; surviving paint and metallic leaf are in-painted to suggest the original effects. Orange silk covers and trim indicate the strong contrast between the original upholstery covers and the frame. According to tradition this chair was part of a set of eight chairs and a settee that descended in a Delaware family from Philadelphia ancestors. The further assertion that they belonged to the Philadelphia financier Robert Morris is now considered to be spurious.[1]

[1] Andrew Passeri and Robert F. Trent, "Some Amazing Washington Chairs! or, White-and-Gold Paint and the Square Stitched Edge," *Maine Antique Digest* 11, no. 4 (May 1983): 1c–3c.

Klismos chair (one of two), 1815–25 ▶
Painted decoration attributed to Hugh Finlay
(w. 1800–1819) or John Finlay (w. 1800–1837)
Baltimore
Cherry, maple, tulip-poplar
H. 31⅝", W. 20⅛", D. 21½"
92.29.1

This exquisite painted version of the ancient Greek klismos chair was part of a set of twelve made for Edward Lloyd (1779–1834) of Wye House, Talbot County, Maryland, the head of the wealthiest plantation family in the state. The Lloyd chairs are one of possibly three sets of Baltimore painted chairs featuring curved front legs in the Greek manner, as opposed to the turned Roman legs seen on all other known sets. The vibrant chrome yellow and chrome green paint scheme is enlivened with gilding, bronzing, and penciling in red, white, black, ochre, and sepia. The seated griffins on the crest are a favorite motif of Baltimore painters and are derived from frieze carvings on the Temple of Antoninus and Faustina, built in Rome in A.D. 141.

▲ Klismos chair (one of nine), 1810–20
Possibly by Joseph B. Barry (w. 1794–d. 1838)
Philadelphia
Rosewood, mahogany, ebony,
ash, white pine, brass
H. 31¾", W. 18⅞", D. 25¾"
88.35.2

This chair is the finest American mahogany version of severe French klismos chairs in the Louis XVI and directoire styles. Chairs of this type have been attributed to Joseph B. Barry on the basis of newspaper ads noting that Barry offered "buhl work," or boulle work, meaning brass inlay. Identical inlay on furniture from New York suggests that Barry was using imported French and English brass, which was widely available. Other variants of this design are decorated with ebony Greek key inlay, intaglio carving of anthemions, or sunken panels. Genealogical research suggests that Winterthur's set of nine chairs belonged to the Hare family of Philadelphia, from whom another large set of twelve identical chairs descended.[1]

[1] J. Michael Flanigan, *American Furniture from the Kaufman Collection* (Washington, D.C.: National Gallery of Art, 1986), pp. 138–39; David B. Warren, *Bayou Bend: American Furniture, Paintings, and Silver from the Bayou Bend Collection* (Houston: Museum of Fine Arts, 1975), p. 94; Chris Ivusic, ed., *Philadelphia: Three Centuries of American Art* (Philadelphia: Philadelphia Museum of Art, 1976), pp. 266–67.

Armchairs, 1735–60
Philadelphia
Walnut, pine; H. 41⅜", W. 32⅝", D. 21¾"
59.2502, 59.2503 Gift of H. F. du Pont

This exquisite pair of severe armchairs epitomizes the fluid lines for which Philadelphia Queen Anne seating is celebrated. Carved ornament is limited to incised lines, shallow shells on the knees, volutes on the forward faces of the arm grips, and lambrequins on the feet. Unusual options are represented by the shaped cabriole legs on the rear posts and the figured walnut veneer on the banisters and the seat rails. Other Philadelphia Queen Anne armchairs are often seen with carved shells, volutes, leafage, and ball-and-claw feet that are considered desirable by collectors but destroy the subtlety of the composition.

Numerous structural features result from the thoughtful layout of this design. The rear posts are pieced on the outer sides above the arms in order to minimize the size of the stock needed to saw them out. The veneered seat rails may have been prompted by the flatwise construction of the seat frame, wherein rails that are broader than they are tall are connected by mortise-and-tenon joints and the front legs are attached with round tenons plugged into the resulting frame. These heavy seat rails greatly increase the weight of the frames, and Philadelphia Queen Anne chairs are prone to damage in the form of broken legs as well as broken arms and chipped edges. Both these chairs have experienced numerous repairs.

Overmantel glass, 1850–60 ▶
New York City
White pine, mahogany, iron, steel, glass,
gesso, gold leaf; H. 65¼", W. 60¼", D. 9½"
91.33

Round, beveled French plate overmantel glasses were perhaps the rarest format for this rococo revival parlor fixture. The titanic scale, extraordinary detailing, and high relief of the composition and carved decoration seen here immediately suggest the eyes and skills of German carvers and gilders, many of whom flooded into New York City after the failed revolution of 1848 in Germany. The exuberant strain of rococo in which these artisans were trained reflected the outer limits of the style as practiced in German cities and principalities throughout the eighteenth century. This example retains its original matte oil gilding with water-gilded highlights. Strong, reflective surface effects were integral to the high-ceilinged rooms in which overmantels, pier glasses, gilt cornices, and other quasi-architectural features were installed.

▲ Pier glass, 1770
Attributed to James Reynolds
(w. 1766–d. 1794), Philadelphia
White pine, tulip-poplar, glass
H. 55½", W. 28¼", D. 3"
52.261 Gift of H. F. du Pont

This is the finest surviving American carved rococo looking glass. It was made for John Cadwalader (1742–86) of Philadelphia as part of a major decorating campaign for his town house. The glass is attributed to the carver James Reynolds on the basis of his bill dated December 5, 1770, which included "To a Pier Glass 36:19 pd. 13 party Gold 18:10.0." The bill, which translates as: charges for a pier glass 36 x 19 inches painted with 13-party gold, £18.10.0, indicates the size of the glass plate and states that the frame was painted white with gilded highlights. Although the surface of the frame is overpainted, it accurately reproduces the original intent. This pier glass and picture frames made for Cadwalader in 1771 form the cornerstone of Reynolds attributions.[1]

[1] Luke Beckerdite, "Philadelphia Carving Shops: Part I, James Reynolds," *Antiques* 125, no. 5 (May 1984): 1120–33; Nicholas B. Wainwright, *Colonial Grandeur in Philadelphia: The House and Furniture of General John Cadwalader* (Philadelphia: Historical Society of Pennsylvania, 1964), pp. 46, 124–25; Morrison H. Heckscher and Leslie Greene Bowman, *American Rococo, 1750–1775: Elegance in Ornament* (New York: Metropolitan Museum of Art, 1992), pp. 186–90.

High chest of drawers, 1750–65
Philadelphia
Mahogany, pine, tulip-poplar, maple
H. 102½", W. 46⅛", D. 24⅝"
57.506 Gift of H. F. du Pont

Dressing table, 1750–65
Philadelphia
Mahogany, pine, tulip-poplar
H. 28½", W. 37", D. 18¾"
57.505 Gift of H. F. du Pont

This magnificent high chest and dressing table were made in the 1750s, but traditionally were created for the 1769 marriage of Michael Gratz (1740–1811) and Miriam Simon (1749–1808), both members of prominent Jewish mercantile families in Philadelphia and Lancaster. The high chest retains its original carved cartouche and burnished Chinese-style brasses, while the dressing table sports original brasses of a different pattern. Close inspection reveals that the structure and the carving of the dressing table were executed by craftsmen other than those who made the high chest, suggesting that the two case pieces were purchased at different times. Both, however, were constructed to appear as if they were made en suite. The work of the unidentified carver of the high chest is extraordinarily elaborate and is picked out with numerous ornamental flourishes and punchwork. The design and execution of the carving differ from the lighter rococo style introduced in Philadelphia by immigrant London-trained carvers after 1763.

Joined chest, dated 1676
Attributed to Thomas Dennis
(w. 1659–d. 1706), Ipswich, Mass.
Red oak, white oak
H. 31¹¹⁄₁₆", W. 49⅝", D. 22⅝"
82.276 Funds for acquisition supplied by
The Honorable Walter H. Annenberg;
Mr. and Mrs. George P. Bissell, Jr.; J. Bruce
Bredin; Mrs. Donald F. Carpenter;
Mrs. Lammot du Pont Copeland; Mrs. Henry
Belin du Pont; John T. Dorrance, Jr.; Mr. and
Mrs. Edward B. du Pont and Mrs. M. Lewis
du Pont; Mrs. Reynolds du Pont; William K.
du Pont; Mrs. George B. Foote, Jr.; Charles J.
Harrington; Mr. and Mrs. George S.
Harrington; Willis F. Harrington; Mr. and
Mrs. Rodney M. Layton; Henry S. McNeil;
Mrs. G. Burton Pearson, Jr.; Stephen A.
Trentman; Mrs. Neal S. Wood

Made for the 1676 marriage of John Staniford
(1648–1730) and Margaret Harris Staniford
(1657–1750) of Ipswich, this is the finest
surviving chest from Thomas Dennis's
joinery shop and arguably the best piece
of seventeenth-century furniture in the
Winterthur collection. Because the chest dates
from a period when Dennis had no recorded
apprentices, and his sons were too young to
have been working, the chest is likely to be
solely Dennis's work. The carved strapwork of
the top rail can be traced to design prints
published in Amsterdam in the 1550s and 1560s.
The red and black painted background of the
carving has been reinforced but is substantially
original.[1]

---

[1] Anthony Wells-Cole, "An Oak Bed at Montacute:
A Study in Mannerist Decoration," *Furniture History* 17
(1981): 1–19; Robert Tarule, "The Joined Furniture of
William Searle and Thomas Dennis: A Shop-Based Inquiry
into the Woodworking Technology of the Seventeenth-
Century Joiner" (Ph.D. diss., Union Institute, 1992).

Easy chair, 1775–90
Philadelphia
Mahogany, oak, maple, white pine, yellow pine, black walnut, tulip-poplar, red gum, linen, iron, horsehair, wool, grass
H. 46⅜", W. 36¼", D. 29½"
92.31

In addition to an outstanding frame with a strong stance and the highest quality carving, this easy chair retains its original upholstery foundation. Like many upholstered objects, it never had fixed covers but was furnished with loose covers that could be changed seasonally. The reproduction loose cover seen here is based on print sources and fragments of slipcovers that survive from the late eighteenth century. The low seat probably never had a stitched hair mattress. The lean, forward edges of the stuffing lead back to heavily stuffed inner areas that make the chair more comfortable and accentuate the splay of the frame. The rarity of original stuffing ensures that this chair will be the standard for anyone interested in Philadelphia upholstered furniture of the rococo period.

Knot bowl, 1775–1825
Attributed to the Woodlands tribes,
eastern United States
Elm, brass; H. 4½", W. 13⅞", D. 12½"
59.1694 Gift of H. F. du Pont

Effigy-carved burl bowls were one of the
major expressive art forms of the Woodlands
tribes and were used for ceremonial purposes.
This example with an animal head em-
bellished with brass nail eyes was found at
Palatine Bridge, New York, in the Mohawk
River valley. Before contact with European
traders, Native Americans made these bowls
by burning and scraping burls, especially elm
burls. Once trading made steel chisels and
knives available, the carving became easier to
execute and perhaps more detailed. The
symbolism of the carved effigy may refer to
clan totems or to the *Midewiwan*, the life-
renewal cult of the Great Lakes tribes that
influenced the Iroquois Confederacy.[1]

[1] Betty Coit Prisch, *Aspects of Change in Seneca
Iroquois Ladles, A.D. 1600–1900* (Rochester, N.Y.: Rochester
Museum and Science Center, 1982).

Miniature high chest of drawers or spice box
1695–1725
Philadelphia
Walnut, cedar, oak, yellow pine
H. 32¹⁵⁄₁₆", W. 21", D. 9½"
88.132 Gift of Mrs. Winifred C. Beer;
Dr. Jane D. Cadbury; John W. Cadbury III;
Elizabeth C. Musgrave; Catherine C. Lambe;
Christopher J. Cadbury; B. Bartram Cadbury;
Joel B. Cadbury; Lloyd Cadbury;
Emma Cadbury; Warder H. Cadbury;
and David F. Cadbury, all the cousins of
Mary Hoxie Jones

A miniature version of a William and Mary high chest of drawers, this spice chest epitomizes the Philadelphia variant of the form. The cases and undercarriage are built of solid walnut rather than being veneered or painted. The turned legs based on bronze Roman prototypes are a style more often seen in Germanic cabinets and suggest the influence of German turners working in Philadelphia. This type of leg, however, is not unknown in England. Six other such spice boxes/high chests are known, but all have either a door on the upper case or a drawer arrangement derived from that of spice boxes rather than high chests.[1] The brass knobs are restored. Some versions of these spice boxes had brass drops and flowered backplates.

[1] Lee Ellen Griffith, *The Pennsylvania Spice Box* (West Chester, Pa.: Chester County Historical Society, 1986), pp. 134–39.

84

High chest of drawers, 1775–90
Attributed to Eliphalet Chapin (1741–1807)
and/or Aaron Chapin (1753–1835)
East Windsor, Conn.
Cherry, white pine; H. 87⅛", W. 40¼", D. 20¼"
93.55 Partial funds for purchase gift of two
anonymous donors

This high chest descended in the King family
of East Windsor from Alexander King
(1749–1831), brother-in-law and cousin-in-law
of the makers. The King family tradition is
that King's own high chest (Garvan
Collection, Yale University Art Gallery) was
made about the time of his marriage in 1781,
but that this example was purchased from a
neighbor in the early 1800s. Other nearly
identical high chests descended in the
Stoughton and Mather families of East
Windsor. Of greatest importance is the
abstract carved cartouche, the only original
example extant and an important sculptural
statement in its own right.

Eliphalet Chapin served journeyman's
time in Philadelphia from 1767 to 1769 and
derived many of his ornamental features from
that experience, but the structure and small
scale of his case pieces relate directly to
Hartford-area design traditions he learned
during his apprenticeship in Suffield or East
Windsor. The apparent scale of high chests
made by Eliphalet and his journeyman and
cousin Aaron is strongly influenced by the
brasses mounted on them; this example has
the original Chinese fret brasses while the
Mather family example (private collection)
has large, solid brasses of a type influenced by
"bat" brasses seen on eighteenth-century
Chinese and Japanese cabinets. The side
finials of high chests and chests-on-chests
from the Connecticut River valley often bear
an unmistakable resemblance to pagodas,
although the means by which these patterns
were transmitted to Connecticut from
England is unclear.

TEXTILES AND EMBROIDERY

DEBORAH E. KRAAK

Textiles surround us from the day of our birth. They provide warmth and protection from the elements, concealment for modesty, and enticement for eroticism. From our earliest experience of soft blankets we retain a tactile attraction to cloth; often our first response to a fabric is to rub it between our fingers. Color also attracts us, as with the rich tones of a cut velvet or the varied hues of an embroidery. We dedicate a large amount of time, money, and thought to acquiring textiles that have been made into clothing that pleases us and attracts or impresses others. In myriad ways textiles—woven, printed, or embroidered—are a major part of our environment. Historically, they have also had great importance because of the costliness of their manufacture in the pre-industrial era, the more abstract quality of beauty of design, and the decorative properties of those ornamented with embroidery. This essay examines these factors and how they come together to create a textile or needlework that is functional and decorative and can also be defined as a masterwork.

Although many people use the criterion of beauty in their definition of a work of art, I feel that it is difficult, if not impossible, to define either the term *beauty* or *art*. Any attempts to be precise or to arrive at an eternal meaning of beauty immediately lead into the shifting territory of personal or cultural taste. The saying "One man's trash is another man's treasure" is no less true in the world of museums, where the deaccessioned collection of one era becomes the prized acquisition of the next. Aside from the indefinite nature of beauty, not everything that is considered a work of art is beautiful. There are paintings, for example, that overwhelm the viewer by virtue of what they communicate of social injustice or moral outrage.

The phrase *work of art* is also subject to endless debate. There is some justification in saying that anything that is fabricated is a work of art, for there is always thought, design, and skill involved. The consciousness of creating a work of art is not necessary to the definition: there are bad paintings by fine artists, excellent paintings by so-called folk artists, sterile professional sculptures, and incredibly powerful African ritual carvings. In addition, many functional objects that are now in museum collections were originally intended for merchants' shelves. Most of the masterworks that I have selected were made by amateur needlewomen, women and young girls who would have been flabbergasted to think of their creations being one day on exhibition in a museum. Yet their works display high standards of craftsmanship and design and communicate something of the taste and personality of those who made them.

It can be difficult to describe why we are moved by a work of art, for the reaction often occurs on an immediate, visceral level without consulting a formal checklist of qualities that must be met. Nevertheless, I feel that the qualities shared by textile and needlework masterpieces are good design, dynamism, individuality, imagination, outstanding technical achievement, and respect for the medium as evidenced in the selection of good materials. Additionally, and almost more important than any other quality, a masterwork must exceed expectations. It is this quality of the unexpected that stops you in your tracks and causes you to take a longer look at the work of art to appreciate it more fully. At its best, this observation becomes a kind of communication between the artist and the viewer, with the latter feeling as though he or she has understood the artist's creative vision and reasons for that particular design or execution. A masterwork speaks with such uniqueness and clarity that it enables the viewer to feel the artist's joy in its creation.

These criteria have been expressed in countless variations across time and cultures. My choice of objects does not attempt to reflect a worldwide survey of textile and needlework masterpieces. The items were drawn from the very focused collections of the museum, which encompass objects either made or used from 1640 to 1860 in what is now the United States of America. The selected objects are largely American embroideries; four textiles were printed in England. All are part of the Anglo-American tradition in the decorative arts that is most representative of the collecting taste of Henry Francis du Pont.

Like other areas of the decorative arts in the museum, the textiles and embroideries are primarily from the eighteenth century and share common stylistic features of that period, such as curving floral branches. This is not to suggest that the line of beauty set up as a paradigm by eighteenth-century English painter William Hogarth is the one and only possible design for a textile or needlework masterpiece. Yet there are a disproportionate number of such designs included here; they reflect the best of the Winterthur collection: samplers, needlework pictures, embroidered panels, and knitted objects.

Both professional and amateur craftspeople are represented in my selections. Only four objects were mass-produced; the rest were made by amateur needlewomen. Different standards for a masterpiece do exist for the professional and the amateur; their training and goals are different. This is not to imply a lower standard for the amateur or a condescension toward the "loving hands at home." Often, greater latitude for personal artistic expression is possible for the amateur. The professional designer of printed or woven textiles or embroidery has to fulfill requirements set by a marketplace that demands a certain level of proficiency in drawing, design, and technology and an adherence to what is considered fashionable by the greatest number of customers. Needlework made by an amateur is free to be completely expressive within the stylistic norms of the day. The works here were made to please a limited number of people: the needleworker, her family, and, to a lesser extent, her community. Within those confines, creativity was given free rein, and great expressive power was the result.

What is called folk art or primitive art has, in the twentieth century, been greatly admired by professional artists who appreciate the vision and genius of an artist with no formal, academic training. Amateur needlework also strikes a chord in many art collectors who hang antique quilts on the wall and appreciate them as they would modern abstract paintings.

Individuality is important in amateur needlework because this is how creativity is expressed. Yet, from what we know about the design of samplers and needlework pictures, individuality might be the last thing we would expect to find. As a rule, specific designs were created by an adult, whether a teacher or a painter or someone else skilled in drawing, and given to schoolgirls to embroider. The stylistic similarities of samplers designed by a particular teacher or in a certain area are what enable scholars to define a school or locale. Within the parameters of a given design and school, however, there are individual variables that break out of the mold of set patterns and models and reveal the personality and enthusiasm of their young creators. Perhaps the choice of colors and types of stitches were left to the embroiderer, making the piece more her own. In formal needlework pictures, the embroiderer's character tends to emerge in the subtle, personal details rather than the technical virtuosity of the embroidery, the elegance of the composition, or the richness of the tints of silk, as beautiful as these may be. This emergence of character is seen in the splendidly designed and skillfully embroidered needlework picture of the tree of life by Mary King, the cover image of this catalogue. A clearer sense of what Mary was like is perhaps more apparent in the less skillfully drawn filling pattern of butterflies that awkwardly dart about the piece or in the choice of a bright blue bead for the lion's eye. Subsidiary details do much to enhance an embroidered picture's originality, and they heighten interest and delight.

Humor is not usually a characteristic of formal embroidery, but it is one of the ways in which the personality of the amateur needlewoman is expressed. If you consider how difficult it is to convey a sense of happiness and mirth through an embroidered image, the accomplishment of the amateur embroiderer becomes even more impressive. Sometimes needlewomen took advantage of the long areas to be filled on crewel-embroidered curtains, valances, or petticoat borders by treating the cloth as a painter's canvas to be covered with a vignette, usually portraying people and animals in a woodland or flowered meadow. The voice that tells the story is the embroiderer's own, and she sometimes enlivens her narrative with comical distortions of perspective, pairing small figures and gigantic birds and flowers or endowing animals with distinctive personalities. A sense of exuberance can be expressed simply by the way in which the landscape itself or the vines and other decorative elements within it rollick in a kind of syncopated rhythm. An embroidery that makes you smile, that gives you a sense of delight, has communicated something about the one who made it.

Outstanding needlework pictures made in the late eighteenth and early nineteenth centuries illustrate a different kind of creativity. Silk-embroidered pictures, or "needle paintings," contrary to the free-style imagery of crewel embroidery, attempt to reproduce a particular printed or painted model. For the needlework to be considered a masterwork it must transcend the mere copying of that model. Many silk pictures are rather bland and pleasant depictions of popular subjects, including scenes from history, literature, and the Bible or mourners at the tomb of George Washington or that of a family member. Instead of functioning as independent works of art, they usually give so strong an impression of being copies that viewer interest in their models can be stronger than an interest in the embroidery itself. Occasionally, however, there will be a masterfully embroidered picture that stuns with its technical virtuosity and freshness. It will contain distinguishing elements, whether in the style and quality of the painting that often defines the sky, faces, and other visible parts of the body or in the individualistic interpretation of the model that is the contribution of the needleworker herself. What might be considered distortions, such as deviations from the source in the treatment of background or drapery, are saving graces if they make a significant contribution to the new mood of the picture as it has been redefined by the embroiderer.

The works described to this point are primarily decorative in character. Most fancy sewing is. Individuality and imagination play nearly as large a role as technical excellence because few functional considerations need to be addressed. On the other hand, in a professionally designed and produced textile, function is critically important, and expertise is essential. Imagination does not exist to delight the designer; it is at the service of the consumer, who constantly requires new images and fresh interpretations of popular subjects. If the designer is so intimately tied to the demands of the marketplace as well as the designated function of the textile, where does creativity enter the picture? The answer is that creativity is necessary if the textile is to exceed the expectations of consumers and the limitations of the medium in which the designer is working.

There are three basic criteria that a commercial, historic textile must meet to be considered excellent. First, it must satisfy the requirements of its function, whether it is to be used for clothing or for furnishings. In other words, it must be well made from the standpoint of technique and technology and, if possible, should be in good condition. Second, no matter what the technique, the design must give the appearance of a continuous, graceful whole instead of a series of repeats of the individual pattern units. Finally, the textile must be well designed.

The first criterion, that of technical expertise, is demonstrated in a variety of ways by the different weaving and printing techniques. One factor all masterfully created textiles share is excellence of materials. Surface quality is especially important for printed cloth. For the textile to be printed successfully, it must be tightly woven, free of dirt and other impurities, and given a smooth surface. The dyestuffs must be of good quality to render a strong, clear color that ideally does not fade easily in the light or run when wet. The tool that is used to make the print must be well cut or engraved, with sharp outlines that clearly define the image. In the case of copperplate prints, the engraving must realize the medium's potential for brilliant, crisp detail. Even a well-engraved plate, however, will lose its sharpness after repeated printings; therefore, a masterwork copperplate-printed textile will come from an early printing. This is a basic criterion for any engraving, including one made on paper. Likewise, a masterwork will have received limited use and exposure to the elements so that the color is still strong and vibrant and makes an appealing contrast with the white of the ground fabric.

The second criterion when discussing the quality of commercially printed textiles deals with the ability of the designer to create a pattern that does not call attention to the limits of the technique used for that design. The shape or size of the woodblocks, copperplate, or roller by which that design is transferred onto cloth must be obscured. A master designer of copperplate-engraved textiles has to create a design that is continuously repeated over countless yards of fabric. His triumph (and most designers were men) is to engrave the 36-by-36-inch plate so that when panels of fabric are sewn together the design appears to interlock and flow seamlessly, both vertically and horizontally. In a sense, to obliterate the awareness of the actual limits of the plate and the selvedges of the textile and to make the design appear to be infinite is a hallmark of the best in printed-textile design.

Last of all, a commercially printed design must be so well conceived that it exemplifies and then transcends an era's standard concept of what is beautiful and demonstrates unexpected artistic possibilities and depth in style. In the case of English printed-textile design from the third quarter of the eighteenth century, a popular fashion included gracefully undulating curves of flowering vines and branches. Pretty bouquets were depicted with a botanical accuracy that let the viewer identify roses, tulips, iris, anemones, daffodils, and any number of popular flowers. It is a charming style, but in the hands of a master designer gracefulness can be combined with a dynamic energy, giving the impression of strength, movement, and growth to the curves. A line is not curving simply because that is the fashion; it is curving with the life force of the plant itself. When a textile design is able to give the feeling that it looks the way it does because of the very nature and spirit of the design itself and not merely as a response or conformation to current fashion, the design is a masterpiece.

The textiles and embroidery presented here all fulfill my personal criteria for a masterwork. Not all masterworks are in museums, however. They also exist in private collections, antiques shops, flea markets, and attics, waiting to be discovered. Made by both the professional and the amateur, they have much to offer of design, artistry, and delight. I urge you to take the time to look for them and at them, to sense the hand of the artist, and to create your own definition of masterwork.

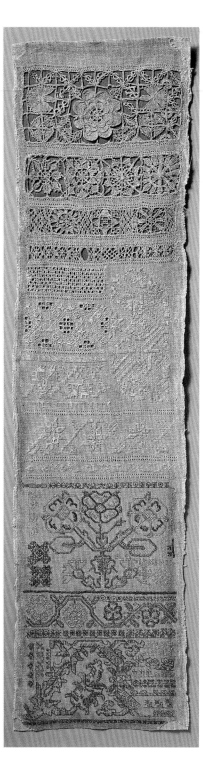

Sampler, 1673
Sarah Collins (possibly Sarah Collens, daughter of Francis and Hanna Collens, b. 1660), Salem, Mass. (?)
Silk yarns embroidered in cross, double running, eyelet, satin, and darning stitches on plain-woven linen; three sets of alphabets and an inscription in satin stitch: "ƨARAH COLLINS HER/ƨAMPLER 1673"; L. 17½", W. 8½"
87.1

Sampler, ca. 1700
Attributed to Mehitable Payson (daughter of Rev. Edward and Elizabeth Phillips Payson, 1688–1773), Rowley, Mass.
Silk and linen yarns embroidered in back, satin, whip, eyelet, buttonhole, weaving, and variations on long-armed cross-stitches on plain-woven linen; bands of drawn work (Dresden work) and cutwork; L. 24", W. 5½"
87.2

Early samplers were a kind of pattern book of a variety of embroidery stitches and motifs that appealed to the needlewoman. Sarah Collins's sampler, with a cool, unified color scheme, suggests that the work was designed with an eye toward its overall appearance. Mehitable Payson's work displays an interest in the various textures that can be achieved with both colored silk and white-on-white embroidery and cutwork and drawn work that includes semidetached flower petals.

Sampler, 1790
Hannah McIntire (1779–1867)
White Clay Hundred,
New Castle County, Del.
Silk yarns embroidered in cross, whip, satin,
eyelet, and chain stitches on plain-woven
linen; inscribed with alphabets, numbers,
and verse; cross stitched inscription:
"HANNAH McINTIERS SAMPLER/MADE IN AUGUST 3
AD 1790/IN THE ELEVENTH YEAR OF HER/AGE"
L. 17 ", W. 12"
93.46

Hannah McIntire's sampler is an exquisite example of late eighteenth-century American embroidery. Although it is a fancy needlework that was meant to be displayed in the family home as a symbol of the education and accomplishments of its maker, it was never framed. This curious fact, in light of the excellent design and workmanship of the piece, accounts for its survival in near pristine condition. In its still-brilliant colors and intact structure it is possible to see an eighteenth-century sampler as it must have looked when it was just made. The sampler is rare for another reason: it is one of four needleworked pieces recently acquired by Winterthur that were made by four generations of a New Castle County, Delaware, family from 1766 to 1850.

Crewelwork panel, 1750–75
Attributed to Mary Dodge Burnham, possibly
Newburyport, Mass.
Crewel yarns embroidered in Roumanian
couching, whip, seed, and satin stitches and
French knots on plain-woven linen
L. 16¼", W. 61⅞"
62.12 Funds for purchase from
the H. F. du Pont funds

In the eighteenth century, particularly in the
New England colonies, women of wealth and
leisure and their school-age daughters embroidered brightly hued patterns on bed
hangings, curtains, and clothing using a type
of wool yarn called crewel.[1] The designer of
this embroidered panel, possibly the
needlewoman herself, showed a highly artistic
sense of color. Scattered accents of yellow,
red, and blue across the entire face of the
embroidery give it great vivacity and sparkle.
Both the lively use of color and the humorous
quality of the picture provide a sense of the
beguiling personality of the individual who
created the piece. But was it designed and
embroidered by one person or two? The
barely perceptible vertical seam that divides

the panel separates two different styles of
design, evident in the thickness and curve of
the meandering vine, the size of the trees and
the way in which their trunks are
embroidered and their roots are depicted, the
number of animals, and the different levels of
sophistication in draftsmanship.

In crewelwork bed hangings or petticoat
borders a sense of whimsy is not uncommon,
but it usually does not appear to the extent
found in this embroidery. There is a "happy,
comical" quality to the piece, largely derived
from the discrepancy between the real and
the depicted size of objects and their juxtaposition.[2] Birds are as large as people; pears
and cherries are gigantic. The rolling terrain
gives a sense of animation that is heightened
by the strong undulations of the floral vine,
echoed in the tightly curved branches of the
fruit trees. Here is joyful abundance. To
quote an inscription on a 1788 American
sampler, "O what a pleasant sight it is to see /
The fruitful Clusters Bowing down the Tree."[3]

[1] Crewel yarns are made of two-ply, loosely twisted
yarns of worsted wool, which is made from the straight,
rather shiny hairs of a sheep's fleece. This gives crewel yarns
a glossy texture.
[2] Susan Burrows Swan, Plain and Fancy: American
Women and Their Needlework, 1700–1850 (New York: Holt,
Rhinehart, and Winston, 1977), p. 145, pl. 29.
[3] For the 1788 sampler inscription, see Ethel
Stanwood Bolton and Eva Johnston Coe, American
Samplers (1921; reprint, New York: Dover Publications,
1987), p. 258.

Canvaswork upholstery, 1725–50
Possibly Boston
Tradition of ownership in the Joshua
Gardner family of Boston
Wool and silk yarns embroidered in cross-
stitch on a linen canvas ground; woven silk
and wool tape binding; reproduction chair
by Winterthur's conservation staff
H. 45⅞", W. 29¼", D. 26"
51.74, 94.500

In 1951 H. F. du Pont acquired a set of
canvaswork upholstery panels that had
been removed from an eighteenth-century
easy chair. For more than forty years

these embroideries were simply part of
Winterthur's extensive collection of colonial
American needlework. The conservation of
the embroidery and the careful recreation of
the original chair now make it possible to
appreciate the embroidery in its original
form and function. Colorful, durable, and
expensive, wool-embroidered chair covers
and slip seats were highly valued in colonial
America for their beauty and quality. This
chair's somewhat reduced scale heightens a
sense of its preciousness. Bright, boldly
drawn flowers, set against a dark blue-green
ground, make the chair resemble a garden.

The embroiderer's selection of these
particular patterns and colors and the careful
execution of the needlework have produced a
beautiful example of the embroiderer's art.

Cushing family coat of arms, ca. 1750
Boston
Probably embroidered by a member of the
Matthew Cushing family of Hingham, Mass.
Silk and crewel yarns embroidered in tent
stitch on linen ground; gold and silver
metallic yarns and lamé worked in couching
stitches and French knots; spangles and glass
beads; L. 22", W. 22"
94.3

One of the most difficult artistic challenges
is the expression of creativity within the
confines of a strictly defined genre. This
embroidered coat of arms demonstrates the
successful completion of just such a challenge.
Like most eighteenth-century coats of arms
made by young women who attended certain
Boston schools, its design, which follows the
formula of a shield topped by a knight's
helmet and surrounded by foliate mantling,
was probably stenciled from a book on
heraldry.[1] Each element of its design is
brilliantly conceived and executed. The use
of tent-stitch embroidery shows evidence
of the young embroiderer's handiwork.
The unusual apple green color, the lavishly
applied gold and silver, which has survived
remarkably untarnished, and the beautiful workmanship all make this a gem
of embroidery.

[1] On the Cushing coat of arms, see Nina Fletcher
Little, *Little by Little: Six Decades of Collecting American
Decorative Arts* (New York: E. P. Dutton, 1984), pp. 137, 145;
Betty Ring, *Girlhood Embroidery*, 2 vols. (New York: Alfred
A. Knopf, 1993), 1:267; Betty Ring, "Heraldric Embroidery
in Eighteenth-Century Boston," *Antiques* 141, no. 4 (April
1992): 622–31.

Pocketbooks, purses, and pincushion
1774–1817
Mary Wright Alsop (1740–1829)
Middletown, Conn.
55.3.3, 55.3.4, 55.3.7, 55.3.11, 55.3.10
Gift of H. F. du Pont

Top left: Knitted pocketbook, 1814; made for her daughter Fanny Alsop (1764–1845); knitted silk yarn with a tension of twenty-one stitches per inch; plain-woven silk binding and tie; lined with warp-printed silk taffeta; a glass-enclosed memorial containing brown hair is fitted inside a small silk pocket in the purse; knitted inscription: (at top) "F·ALSOP 1814"; (at bottom) "M·ALSOP 74"
H. 4⅝" (closed), W. 4⅝"

Top right: Embroidered pocketbook, 1774; silk yarns embroidered in queen's stitch on linen canvas; striped silk tape binding; lined with striped plain-woven silk; cross stitched inscription: "Mary + Alsop 1774"
H. 3½" (closed), W. 5¾"

Bottom left: Knitted pincushion, 1790–1800; knitted silk yarn with a tension of twenty-two stitches per inch; silk ribbon binding; backed with warp-printed silk taffeta; H. 4⅜", W. 3"

Bottom center: Knitted drawstring purse, 1812; made for her son John Alsop (1776–1841); knitted silk yarn with a tension of twenty-six stitches per inch; trimmed with silk, silk chenille, and metallic yarns; knitted inscription: "JOHN ALSOP 1812 M + A"
L. 8⅛", W. 3⅞"

Bottom right: Knitted drawstring purse, 1817; made for her daughter Clarissa Alsop Pomeroy (1770–1852); knitted silk with a tension of twenty-two stitches per inch; lined with plain-woven silk and kidskin; trimmed with silk, silk chenille, and metallic yarns; knitted inscription: "C: ALSOP 1817 M: A 77"
L. 6¼", W. 3"

Embroidered and knitted purses, pocketbooks, and pincushions were among the many day-to-day objects upon which colonial women lavished their care and skill. Those shown here are a selection from the large body of surviving needlework made by Mary Wright Alsop. As a young girl, wife, mother, widow, and grandmother, she produced an astonishing array of brilliantly colored and beautifully worked pieces.[1] Her knitted objects are technically remarkable and visually dazzling. Made with extremely fine needles, some have twenty-seven stitches per inch. Mary Alsop took advantage of the fineness of the knitting to make subtle gradations of color in the geometric, mosaic-like motifs. As many as twenty colors are used to give the forms an illusion of three dimensionality.

---

[1] Glee Krueger, "A Middletown Cameo: Mary Wright Alsop and Her Needlework," *Connecticut Historical Society Bulletin* 52, nos. 3–4 (Summer/Fall 1987): 125–227. Swan, *Plain and Fancy*, pl. 20.

Needlework picture, 1754
Mary King, Philadelphia
Silk and metallic yarns and glass beads
embroidered in satin, whip, seed, and
couching stitches on silk moiré; embroidered
inscription in metallic yarns below the
leopard's forepaw: "1754/MARY KING"
L. 18¼", W. 24⅛"
66.978 Bequest of H. F. du Pont

A distinctive style of needlework picture made
with silk yarns on a silk ground fabric was
characteristic of mid eighteenth-century
Philadelphia. Yellow moiré (or watered silk)
is the background selected for Mary King's
picture of a tree of life. Its curving branches
display a luxuriant array of blossoms that are
rendered with skillful shadings of silk

embroidery and highlighted with metallic
yarns. There is a jewel-like brilliance in the
strong contrast among the crimsons, pinks,
and blues of the flowers and the deep yellow
of the silk that sets this embroidery apart from
other Philadelphia examples of the same
period. Although imported Indian fabrics
may have supplied the inspiration for the
bizarre flowers and the overall composition
was probably the handiwork of a teacher, the
personality and artistry of the embroiderer is
evident throughout the piece.[1]

---

[1] Susan Burrows Swan, *A Winterthur Guide to
American Needlework* (New York: Crown Publishers, 1976),
pl. 11.

Lace sampler, 1795
Philadelphia
Cutwork and drawn work (Dresden work);
silk yarns embroidered in whip, satin, cross,
chain, and detached buttonhole stitches and
French knots on plain-woven linen; cross-
stitch inscription: "MS/1795"
L. 11¾", W. 14½"
92.65

Lace was the most costly fashion accessory of
the eighteenth century, often more valuable
than the article it decorated. It was so
desirable that people went to great lengths to
acquire exquisite bobbin lace or to imitate its
fragile beauty by less-expensive means.
Several methods of creating lace are used in
this sampler, and each requires extraordinary
patience and skill on the part of the
embroiderer. The low flower basket and most
of the medallions within the flowers are made

in drawn work or, to use the period term,
Dresden work, named for the German city
associated with this technique. Certain warp
and weft threads are removed from sections of
the ground fabric, and embroidery stitches
draw the remaining threads together into
lacelike designs with a characteristic grid
structure. Cutwork designs, seen here in the
roundels, are more free form, since the
embroiderer could use her needle to fill in a
cutout section with variations of the
buttonhole stitch. These techniques are
combined here with colorful silk embroidery
of stylized flowers, leaves, and bows. The
harmonious balance of lace and embroidery,
curving lines, and rounded forms elicits, as it
was intended to, admiration for the skill and
artistry of the embroiderer.[1]

---

[1] Swan, *Plain and Fancy*, pp. 225–26.

Bed rug, 1778
Mary Foot (1752–1837), Colchester, Conn.
Wool yarns embroidered in running and
darning stitches on plain-woven wool; wool
fringe woven separately on a tape loom;
embroidered inscription: "MARY FOOT AD
1778"; L. 77", W. 77½"
60.594 Bequest of H. F. du Pont

Although bed rugs were used in many early
American homes, where they provided both
warmth and beauty, few have survived.
These rare examples illustrate bold designs
achieved using a limited range of materials
and techniques—wool embroidery that
completely covers the foundation fabric.
Nowhere is the result of an imagination
flourishing within the constraints of the
medium more successful than in this bed rug
by Mary Foot, probably made for her
November 5, 1778, marriage to the Reverend
David Huntington. Only a few colors and
stitches are used, but what diversity of design
is achieved. Over nineteen separate
patterns—perhaps taken from fabric weaves,
coverlet patterns, and quilting stitches—fill
the floral and leaf motifs: diamonds, trellis
patterns, checks, parallel lines, triangles, and
zigzags.[1] Dazzling complexity, balanced by
the restraint of the floral design and the
selected colors, produces a bed rug that looks
light and graceful rather than weighty and
awkward.

[1] On the Foot family, see Abram W. Foote, *Foote
Family: Comprising the Genealogy and History of Nathaniel
Foote of Wethersfield, Connecticut, and His Descendants*, 2
vols. (Rutland, Vt.: Tuttle Co., 1907), 1:48. According to
Ruth Page, the Foot girls also carded, spun, and wove
wool, made quilts, and wove coverlets; Ruth Page to
Florence Montgomery, January 25, 1967, collection notes,
Registration Division, Winterthur. For more on bed rugs,
see J. Herbert Callister and William L. Warren, *Bed Ruggs,
1722–1833* (Hartford, Conn.: Wadsworth Atheneum, 1972),
pp. 17, 18, no. 19.

103

Liberty, in the Form of the Goddess of Youth, Giving Support to the Bald Eagle, embroidered picture, 1796–1820; United States; after a Chinese painted version of an engraving of the lost painting of the same title by Edward Savage, 1796
Paint, spangles, silk, silk chenille, and metallic yarns; embroidered in satin stitches on plain-woven silk; L. 22⁷⁄₁₆", W. 18¾"
69.1790 Bequest of H. F. du Pont

In 1796 the painter Edward Savage (1761–1817) published an engraving based on his oil painting *Liberty, in the Form of the Goddess of Youth, Giving Support to the Bald Eagle.* It was a popular subject for embroidered pictures, which followed their models with varying degrees of fidelity. This version is one of the most exciting. If the original oil was romantic, with its allegorical portrayal of America aiding the eagle of freedom, the embroidered picture is sublime, with all of the heightened emotions of ecstasy and terror that the movement espoused. Various elements of the composition have been skillfully altered with a keen sense of the dramatic to heighten a sense of excitement. The dark, roiling clouds that dominate two-thirds of the scene, although not expertly painted, set the tone. They look as if they are being compressed by a field of energy pushing in from the right side of the picture. Everything seems to crackle with some interior electricity, manifested in the woman's spiky coiffure, the glitter of the spangles on her dress, the exaggerated spires of the buildings in the distance, and the way in which the tree branches seen over the left horizon seem to whirl like the teeth of a buzz saw. The quality of the painted parts of the picture does not equal the finesse of the embroidery; rather than detract from the work, this complements the vigor of the embroidered representation. The model has been transcended; an independent work of art has been created.

Textile panel, 1765–75
Designed by Francis Nixon (w. 1752–d. 1765)
for Nixon and Co., Phippsbridge (near
Merton), Surrey, England
Copperplate printed on plain-woven cotton
L. 104½", w. 36"
69.3889.3 Bequest of H. F. du Pont

Countless yards of printed textiles were
manufactured in England during the
eighteenth century to satisfy the public's
enthusiasm for colorfully patterned, lightweight cotton and linen fabrics. This
furnishing fabric is one of the most beautiful
in its design and execution. A high-water
mark of English copperplate textile printing,
it was designed by Francis Nixon, the
probable initiator of copperplate printing on
cloth.[1] A strongly curving central branch sets
the basic visual rhythm, with graceful
counterpoint provided by the serrated leaves
and the sprays of flowers that arch from the
main stem. So expertly balanced is the design
that it is pleasing from any point of view,
whether right side up, upside down, or
sideways—not an insignificant consideration
for upholstery fabric. The engraver realized
the design with consummate skill. The
excellent quality of the engraving is evident in
this length of fabric, which must have been
printed from a newly engraved plate, before
successive impressions blurred the image.
The clean, cool contrast of the relatively
unfaded indigo on the white ground allows
us to appreciate the original impact of
this textile.

[1] Florence M. Montgomery, *Printed Textiles: English and American Cottons and Linens, 1700–1850* (New York: Viking Press, 1970), fig. 215, pp. 231–32.

Textile panel, 1831
Lancashire, England
Roller printed on plain-woven cotton; stripes
of acanthus scrolls containing stars
H. 12½", W. 16⅝"
59.84.29 Gift of the Victoria
and Albert Museum

Textile panel, 1834
Lancashire, England
Roller printed on plain-woven cotton; over-
printed in green; floral garlands on mauve
with trellis pattern
H. 17¾", W. 25¼"
59.84.15 Gift of the Victoria
and Albert Museum

Textile panel, 1837
England
Roller printed on plain-woven cotton; over-
printed in green; paisley scrolls and flowers
on tan
H. 17⅞", W. 24"
59.84.46 Gift of the Victoria
and Albert Museum

Taste preference in color, pattern, and density
of design change over time. What is seen as
chic and stylish in one era can be regarded as
vulgar and garish in another. These three
English furnishing textiles of the 1830s are a
case in point. When they were produced they
were very fashionable. Their brilliant colors
and mixture of patterns appealed to the early
Victorians. Those same characteristics were
later seen as being disturbing and chaotic.
Taste has once again changed, and the textiles'
eclectic mixture of geometric and floral
patterns and juxtaposition of saturated
colors are currently appreciated. The skillful combination of strong elements may,
to the modern eye, be their most exciting characteristic.[1]

---

[1] Montgomery, *Printed Textiles*, figs. 365, 366.

PAINTINGS
AND PRINTS

E. McSHERRY FOWBLE

By its strictest definition a masterpiece, or masterwork, is proof that its maker has attained the skills of design and execution required of a master of the craft. Over the centuries the term has taken on the connotation of unrivaled excellence and has been applied generally to outstanding examples of art, whenever executed in the maker's career. Such criteria as technique, quality of materials, and beauty of design have all been brought to bear in justifying a masterpiece. Excellence in workmanship that exhibits both control of technique and a thorough understanding of the properties of the materials is prerequisite. Carrying this control and understanding to its farthest limits characterizes an eye for infinite detail that is essential to achieving the extraordinary in fabrication. By far the most elusive and most emotional quality of a masterwork is beauty, and yet it is the most obvious. We each have our own standards for beauty. On occasion, following in the footsteps of Andrew Jackson, we dismiss our choices with the disclaimer that "I don't know anything about art, but I know what I like." On other occasions we may justify our choices from a wide menu of reasons, some as direct as "It just appeals to me," or as purposeful as "Its color goes best in this room," or as obtuse as "I find the tensions between the broad expanses of vibrant color and the diagonal arrangement of the design to be dynamic."

Henry Francis du Pont found color and line to be exhilarating and used both to define his very genius. They are evident in his gardens and in the museum rooms he assembled. But while color and line are the essential elements of the painter's and engraver's work, du Pont had only a passing interest in paintings or prints. He considered them as parts in the entire room assemblage. Once he wrote to a dealer about a painting he was considering for purchase: "I have decided to keep the picture. . . . As it fits a certain place I would be foolish to let it go by. I am looking for another picture just that size and shape, and if you should come across one, will you be good enough to let me know."[1] Du Pont was just as deliberately motivated in his selection of prints for the collection and arranged his acquisitions in rooms according to a theme that was apropos to the surrounding architecture and objects. He was most satisfied when pictures on the wall melded into the theme of the room as established by the furniture and other decorative arts.

Beginning at a time when the academic discipline of American painting and the study of prints pertaining to America were in their nascent stages, du Pont relied on his instincts and succeeded in acquiring what have proved to be a number of monuments in American art. In succeeding years museum directors and curators have moved to widen and deepen the collection of paintings and prints. It is from this very catholic assemblage that I have selected twelve paintings and graphic masterpieces as the best of their kind.

Color and line (or form in three-dimensional objects), mastery of technique, and attention to details are universal measurements of excellence for artisan and artist alike. Unlike most artisans, the artist and engraver fulfill the role of historian or chronicler and bring insights that come from an intense understanding of a particular time and place. To my mind what distinguishes a masterwork from the ordinary painting or print is the artist's ability to capture this insight and the energies of the moment and to preserve them for succeeding generations. My focus has been foremost on the artist's ability to translate the energies of a time and place onto canvas, panel, or paper with such vigor and cognition that it brings to the present the vitality, philosophy, and spirit of that individual's world. As a result, this selection touches upon significant artistic trends as they appeared in America from the early 1700s to 1850.

Samuel Johnson wrote in the *Idler* (no. 45) for February 24, 1759: "It is in painting as in life; what is the greatest is not always the best." Living in England at a time when history painting and classical metaphors were the mark of artistic genius, Johnson was wrestling with the notion that the popular art of portraiture was somehow compromised by the fleeting fame or obscurity of its subjects. While raising the issue of merit, Johnson was also addressing issues of sentiment, taste, and technical accomplishment: "I should grieve to see Reynolds transfer to heroes and to goddesses, to empty splendor and to airy fiction, that art which is now employed in diffusing friendship, in reviving tenderness, in quickening the affections of the absent, and continuing the presence of the dead."

Until the 1760s portraiture dominated the development of English painting, and English art remained the principal influence on American art well into the nineteenth century. Since the seventeenth century the portrait had been widely accepted in America as a perpetual homage to an individual and a worthy pursuit of the artist.[2] Landscapes, copies after Italian masters, and the occasional allegorical subject as well as other decorative pieces appeared in colonial homes from the seventeenth century, but on a minor scale before the early nineteenth century.

British and European-trained painters, who slowly but steadily arrived in America, provided rudimentary training for aspiring colonial talents, and an expanding importation of European engravings served the colonial artist and the patron as well. It was the portrait, whether painted in London or in the colonies, that defined painting in America until the 1790s.

The colonial population was largely focused on work: work to become established and work to survive. Although there was the element of an upwardly mobile society, America lacked the sizeable gentry necessary to attract leading European artists. Those painters and printmakers who did emigrate were of modest talents. Nonetheless, handbooks written during the seventeenth and eighteenth centuries about the techniques and mysteries of drawing, painting, and engraving as well as treatises on art history and theory were available to inform the colonial practitioner and the learned patron alike.[3]

John Singleton Copley (1738–1815) grew up in the midst of Boston's art trade. His stepfather, Peter Pelham (1697–1751), had been a modestly successful mezzotint engraver in London before coming to Boston in 1727. A year later the Edinburgh portrait painter John Smibert also came to Boston, bringing with him a collection of engravings and his own copies in oil of the Italian masters. These copies and the ever-increasing number of European engravings available in Boston served Copley as models for tonal color (chiaroscuro) as well as technique and composition.[4] With contemporary treatises on art and the tutelage of Smibert and others, Copley progressed from the stilted likenesses of his earlier years to a luscious rococo style and formula that he used repeatedly in both his portraits in oil and in the deceptively difficult medium of pastel, or crayon, that he chose for his self-portrait. Copley, however, was driven to exceed both the accomplishments of his contemporaries and his own sizeable achievements. It was not enough to be recognized as the best in America, to succeed he had to study and compete within the principal artistic arenas of Rome and London. He sailed from Boston for Europe in 1774 and settled in London in 1776. He left behind in America a vivid record of colonial gentility.

Two of the leading voices in English painting of the eighteenth century argued that portraiture was at its best if it *exceeded* the limits of likenesses. Jonathan Richardson (1665–1745) challenged artists to avoid an otherwise "Company of Awkward, and Silly-looking People" by raising the common visage that nature bestowed to "an Abstract of one's life." Joshua Reynolds (1723–92) observed in 1771, however, that "it is very difficult to ennoble the character of a countenance but at the expense of likeness."[5]

Benjamin West (1738–1820) was the first American-born artist to leave for Europe and three years of study in Italy and to see firsthand the achievements of the Renaissance and baroque artists. He never returned to America but chose to establish a studio in London in 1763 that, for the next four decades, served as a major base for many American artists in search of a deeper understanding of the craft to which they aspired.

Charles Willson Peale (1741–1821), one of the first Americans to visit West in London, has been acclaimed for his more complex multifigural compositions and his heroic military portraits. With the portrait of Richard Bennett Lloyd the artist seems equal to the challenges of Richardson and Reynolds. In this one painting Peale combines the counterpoint of the late baroque style with clear references to the neoclassical taste then endorsed by the cognoscenti in London but not yet widely understood in America.

Although pastels, oil colors, and watercolors each have their own distinct characteristics, in the hand of a master any medium can be pushed to its limits and otherwise manipulated to produce startling effects. The remarkable effect of luminosity that Copley achieved in his pastels Thomas Sully (1783–1872) succeeded in capturing in many of the portraits he executed in oil following an 1809/10 visit to London and his acquaintance with the work of London's leading portraitist, Sir Thomas Lawrence (1769–1830). Upon his return to Philadelphia, Sully quickly gained prominence as the city's leading portrait painter. With rapid, sure brush strokes and a vivid palette he portrayed his male subjects as handsome, romantic, and virile. His ladies were elegant, sensitive, and soft, as if painted with air and light. Little wonder that Sully was the likely choice of the newly wealthly intent upon establishing themselves in polite Philadelphia society in the first decades of the nineteenth century.

Pictures depicting flowers and fruit appear sporadically in American inventories during the last quarter of the seventeenth century. After 1750 travelers from abroad noted in their journals that they had seen old Dutch pictures (religious and mythological) as well as flower pieces in American homes. Numerous references are made in personal and business records to imported engraved pictures of flowers, fruits, and vegetables in America. Many such compositions of flowers and vegetables were arranged as metaphors on the inherent frailties of life, subject matter that appealed to a small number of artists from the seventeenth century. Designers saw decorative possibilities in such arrangements. Robert Sayer, in the mid eighteenth century, used engravings of floral compositions to teach young artists the fundamentals of decoration in *The Ladies Amusement*.[6] By the 1770s remarkable subjects employing still-life arrangements, some taken from paintings made in Europe a century earlier, were being engraved and printed in colors and black and white for the British and American markets.

Living in Philadelphia, James Peale (1749–1831) undoubtedly had access to such engravings, and he actually may have seen seventeenth- or early eighteenth-century originals or copies of Dutch still-life paintings in some of the larger private collections in the city.[7] He knew of John Bartram's work as America's leading botanist and of his brother Charles Willson Peale's gardens at Belfield. More importantly, he witnessed the work of his nephew Raphaelle Peale (1774–1825)—a gifted painter and the first artist in America to use still-life painting as a vehicle for expression and an illusion for life's larger meanings. For James Peale, however, still-life paintings were primarily a new challenge in composition, color, and textures—one in which he could succeed even after diminished eyesight ended his career as a painter of miniature portraits.

The Society of Artists in the United States held their first annual exhibition in rooms of the Pennsylvania Academy of the Fine Arts in Philadelphia in 1811. "Dare to have sense your selves" was the challenge that they lay before gallery visitors on the title page of the catalogue. For the first time, Philadelphians could see and *buy* drawings, paintings, and sculpture by contemporary artists in a space adjacent to permanent galleries filled with works by or after European masters and collections of casts from the antique. The 1811 exhibition included nineteen entries for still-life compositions, either fruits or flowers, but the largest single group of paintings were landscapes, forty-nine in all, and each was for sale. Among these were several views of the area's country houses, by newly arrived English landscape painters. Among the new gentry it was becoming as fashionable to have a portrait of one's house painted as it was to have a portrait of oneself. In the best of house portraits the life-styles of its occupants permeated the image, and within these can be found the beginnings of genre painting in America.

Samuel Finley Breese Morse (1791–1872) made his second trip to Italy not as a student but as an established master in search of greater understanding of the old masters. As founder and president of the National Academy of Design, teacher of painting, lecturer on art theory, and New York's most respected cultural figure, Morse was among the most prominent and recognized of American artists.[8] When he left New York in November 1829, he was traveling to Italy on funds provided by subscriptions for copies of old masters or original designs placed by leading patrons of the arts, including Dr. David Hosack. For his contribution of $300, Hosack asked for two cabinet-sized paintings of the artist's own invention.

Abroad, Morse was forced to confront his own feelings regarding the cultural and artistic richness and eloquence of Europe as it contrasted with what he saw as the abuse of the "squalid masses."[9] In the galleries he studied the palette and techniques of Titian, Rubens, Tintoretto, and others, and he kept detailed notes of his observations in diaries. While specific copies demanded by his New York patrons allowed Morse the opportunity to learn through imitation, Hosack's commission provided the artist with a chance to apply what he had discovered in old masterpieces to his own artistic statement. He chose the theme of the Roman Catholic church versus the common man in *Pifferai* and its pendant *The Brigand Alarmed*.

Like American painting of the seventeenth and eighteenth centuries, the development of colonial printmaking depended largely upon the talents of those recently arrived from England or the Continent. Like the colonial artists who found it necessary to perform many jobs, including sign painting, to earn a living, colonial engravers were frequently engaged in several businesses.

William Burgis (w. in America 1718–31) is known as an engraver from one map and nine landscape or topographical views: a great prospect of the city of New York, one view of Fort George, and the rest in and around Boston. In 1729 he designed and engraved *View of the Lighthouse*, in Boston. It is a remarkable production, not only for being what is regarded as the first American engraving of a maritime subject but for the use of mezzotint, a tonal technique invented in the mid seventeenth century and most often applied to portraiture.[10]

Burgis appears to have escaped the economic necessity of producing designs and copperplates for the more ordinary productions associated with commerce and government. Most eighteenth-century American engravers were less fortunate and found themselves supplying engraved designs for anything from billheads and bookplates to currency and official seals. James Smither (d. 1797) came from England to Philadelphia and advertised as an engraver in *The Pennsylvania Journal* of 1768. Smither's talents as an engraver were particularly appreciated in the cosmopolitan atmosphere of Philadelphia, where merchants such as Robert Kennedy and

Benjamin Randolph were intent upon providing goods and services equal to those found in London. In his trade cards for Kennedy, Randolph, and others, Smither introduced to American engraving the full-blown elegance and delight of the rococo style.

Paul Revere was a silversmith who initially learned the art of engraving as a means of ornamentation. In the volatile climate of Boston, from the imposition of the Stamp Act of 1765 through the signing of the peace treaty with England in 1783, Revere the patriot applied his burin to subjects possessing an interesting combination of historical reporting and political incitement. He borrowed liberally from English sources, often changing his copy only by returning the satirical abuse with a few clever additions or omissions. On rare occasions Revere produced original pictorial designs of great power. His straightforward, carefully detailed recording of the obelisk erected in Boston in 1766 in celebration of the repeal of the Stamp Act is a powerful record of popular sentiment in a city where citizens saw themselves as Englishmen abroad, not just faceless, nameless workers serving the king's treasury.

From the sixteenth century, artists have understood the advantages in combining their talents with those of the printmaker, not the least of which was the ability to spread their fame and realize financial reward. This collaboration became increasingly important in the eighteenth century as larger markets demanded excellent engravings for framing. In most cases the artist relied on a professional engraver. In exceptional cases the artist *was* the engraver. John Singleton Copley and Charles Willson Peale were two American artists who experimented with printmaking. More often, an artist would begin his career as an engraver before turning to painting. In America the most accomplished line engraver was Asher Brown Durand (1796–1886), who took his apprenticeship with Peter Maverick of New York City and improved at his craft so quickly that he was asked to become a partner. Durand was driven by his vision of carrying his execution beyond a merely satisfactory reproduction to the level of art itself. His work was regarded highly by contemporary artists, and he was elected to the National Academy of Design.

To choose a masterwork, what is best in art, is to offer one opinion, to elicit a response, and occasionally to stimulate controversy. Such choices, whether widely supported or unequivocally challenged, succeed not because they are right or wrong but because they make us explore our own reactions, our own ideas. Art is *not* just decoration, it is communication. What is best in art is highly subjective, for it is an evaluation not merely of the technical proficiency of the artist but of the artist's ability to convey the essence of an idea and a time to contemporaries and to successive generations. Each of the works of art that follow meets these criteria for me and in so doing have provoked me most emphatically to reconsider a time long past. I hope they will succeed in opening a window to the past for you as well.

[1] H. F. du Pont to Miss Eunice Chambers, Hartsville, S.C., February 3, 1930, Du Pont correspondence, Registration Division, Winterthur.

[2] Jonathan Fairbanks, "Portrait Painting in Seventeenth-Century Boston: Its History, Methods, and Materials," in *New England Begins: The Seventeenth Century*, 3 vols. (Boston: Museum of Fine Arts, 1982), 3:421–22.

[3] Janice G. Schimmelman, "Books on Drawing and Painting Techniques Available in Eighteenth-Century American Libraries," *Winterthur Portfolio* 19, nos. 2/3 (Summer/Autumn 1984): 193–205; Janice G. Schimmelman, "A Checklist of European Treatises on Art and Essays on Aesthetics Available in America through 1815," *Proceedings of the American Antiquarian Society* 93 (April 1983): 95–190.

[4] Richard H. Saunders and Ellen G. Miles, *American Colonial Portraits, 1700–1776* (Washington, D.C.: Smithsonian Institution Press for the National Portrait Gallery, 1987), p. 114.

[5] Jonathan Richardson, *An Essay on the Theory of Painting* (London, 1715), pp. 172–73. Sir Joshua Reynolds, *Discourses on Art*, ed. Robert R. Wark (1797; reprint, New Haven, Conn.: Yale University Press, 1975), p. 72.

[6] From the seventeenth century, learned circles, particularly in London, considered still life at the bottom in the hierarchy of subjects worthy of an artist's efforts; see Nicolai Cikovsky, Jr., *Raphaelle Peale Still Lifes* (Washington, D.C.: National Gallery of Art, 1988), pp. 31–71. Robert Sayer, *The Ladies Amusement; or, Whole Art of Japanning Made Easy* (2d ed., 1762; reprint, London: Ceramic Book Co., 1959).

[7] Carington Bowles, *The Art of Painting in Water-Colours; Exemplified in Landscapes, Flowers, &c.* (8th ed.; London, 1786) contains pictures of fruits (apples, pears, and peaches), vegetables, and seventy different varieties of flowers. Subsequent editions of 1788, 1797, 1802, 1818, and 1839 underscore the lasting popularity of this source for amateurs and artists.

[8] Paul Staiti, *Samuel F. B. Morse* (Cambridge, Eng.: Cambridge University Press, 1989), pp. 175, 126, 176.

[9] Staiti, *Morse*, p. 176.

[10] Richard B. Holman, "William Burgis," in *Boston Prints and Printmakers*, 1670–1775, ed. Walter Whitehill and Sinclair Hitchings (Boston: Colonial Society of Massachusetts, 1973), pp. 57–81. Peter Pelham was the first to practice mezzotint engraving in the colonies. As both he and Burgis were practicing printmakers, it is certain that they would have known each other. Pelham may have instructed Burgis in mezzotint. See Holman, "William Burgis," pp. 71–72.

Self-portrait of John Singleton Copley, 1769
Boston
Pastel on laid paper, mounted on canvas
(unsigned); H. 23⅛", W. 17½"
58.1127a Gift of H. F. du Pont

In his ambition to discover all that he could about the arts of painting and drawing Copley tried various techniques and media including pastels, or crayons as they were known in his time. Crayon is demanding of the artist and generally unforgiving of mistakes. Unlike oil painting, where colors can be applied over colors in multiple layers, the amount of pastel that can be held by the support (usually a strong, rough-textured paper, which in the eighteenth century was stretched taut onto a canvas backing) is limited to the depth, or tooth, of the paper surface. While judicious use of a fixing agent can stabilize base colors, excessive amounts of pigment produce dull, pastelike results. When best executed, pastels retain an iridescence and fragility that seem to bathe the subject in light. Copley remarked of pastels: "I think my best portraits [are] done in that way."[1]

In 1769, the year of the artist's marriage to Susanna Clarke, daughter of a wealthy and prominent merchant of Boston, Copley executed a self-portrait and one of his bride in pastel. Poised and elegant in powdered wig and a damask banyan opened to reveal an elaborate waistcoat, Copley glances from just the other side of the picture plane. The casual viewer may be quick to believe that Copley is glancing sidelong at him or her and not realize that the artist is actually looking at himself as he paints his image from a reflection in the looking glass.

With his marriage, Copley firmly established his place in Boston society. His position as the city's leading artist was undisputed. This portrait, with its casual but assured air, attests to his status as a gentleman. It is interesting that in choosing the size for this portrait, Copley selected the conservative, smaller format that had been popular among old Boston society since the 1740s.

[1] Copley was certainly not the first artist working in America to use pastel in the execution of portrait commissions. Henrietta Dering Johnston (d. 1729) was working in America around 1708–25; see Margaret Simons Middleton, *Henrietta Johnston of Charlestown, South Carolina, America's First Pastellist* (Columbia: University of South Carolina Press, 1966). Carington Bowles's volume *The Artist's Assistant* (London, 176?) offered instruction in drawing, perspective etching, engraving, mezzotinto scraping, painting on glass, crayons, and watercolors, providing the earliest and most comprehensive rules. *Letters and Papers of John Singleton Copley and Henry Pelham, 1739–1776* (Boston: Massachusetts Historical Society, 1914), p. 51.

Portrait of Richard Bennett Lloyd, 1771
Charles Willson Peale, London Town,
the Stewart home near Annapolis, Md.
Oil on canvas (unsigned); H. 48", W. 36⅛"
62.590 Gift of H. F. du Pont

Charles Willson Peale wrote to John Beale Bordley from London soon after his arrival in 1767. "Mr. West . . . gives me Encouragement to pursue my Plan of Paintg. and Promises me all the Instruction he is capable of giving."[1] Peale's career as an artist owed much to the early support he received from patrons like Bordley and the Lloyds of Maryland. With their financial help he had a firsthand opportunity to meet with some of England's leading painters. The impact of this experience lent a presence to Peale's later portrait commissions that fit well into his wealthy patrons' self-images. Richard Lloyd and his brother, Edward, were among the first to sit for Peale upon his return to Maryland in 1769. While Edward, in a characteristic familial gesture, chose to sit with his wife and daughter, Richard, as a bachelor and gallant, quite nonchalantly assumed the pose of Apollo Belvedere, a classical masterpiece widely recognized in the eighteenth-century Western world and understood by many young men who pursued the classics as part of their basic education.

In imitating the antique, Richard stands resting his weight on his right arm as he leans against a plinth. He deliberately looks away from the viewer as though occupied in deep thought. He is dressed elegantly. His head and right side are brilliantly contrasted against dark green foliage, while his left profile is silhouetted against a distant landscape with waterfall. For the moment Lloyd seems to be still, but given the diagonal division of the composition and the tensions it suggests, the viewer is reminded of the momentary nature of the scene and is left with the hint that the subject, without notice, will rise and walk away.

[1] Lillian B. Miller, ed., *The Selected Papers of Charles Willson Peale and His Family*, 2 vols. (New Haven, Conn.: Yale University Press, 1983), 1:47–48.

Portrait of Mrs. Benjamin Tevis
(Mary M. Hunter), 1827
Thomas Sully, Philadelphia
Oil on canvas (signed lower left "TS 1827")
H. 30", W. 25"
75.115.2a

Benjamin Tevis engaged Thomas Sully to paint his portrait in 1822; in 1827 he employed the artist to paint a companion portrait of his wife of three years, Mary Hunter Tevis (d. 1869), daughter of the late William Hunter of Philadelphia. We know very little of Mary Hunter Tevis except through the artist's eye.

Sully's technique was greatly admired in his own time. One writer remarked that "he exhibits the freedom of touch and the airiness of outline which belong to spontaneous emanations."[1] Sully painted more than 2,000 portraits in his long career. He followed the practice of making a quick sketch on paper during the first sitting to show the client and to discuss any changes. Between then and the second sitting he worked out a full-size sketch using black and white chalk on a gray grounded canvas. This could readily be changed at the beginning of the second sitting. During the second session he initiated the principal portrait, beginning with umber washes rapidly sketched on a white grounded canvas. At the third sitting he began to apply colors quickly and freely, with certainty and elegance. In Sully's portraits, focus is on the face, the light, and the personality of his subject. Others among his contemporaries executed the human anatomy with greater

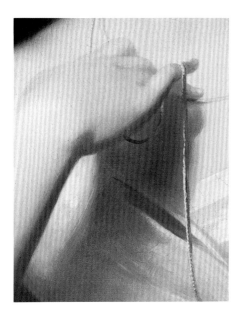

structure and substance, but none exceeded Sully's ability to capture a moment in his subject's life.

Unlike eighteenth-century sitters who favored the timeless, loosely fitting draped gown, neoclassical or otherwise, Mary Tevis chose the latest of fashions, a dress with puffed sleeves and a high waist belted in gold. Sully's portrait is executed with broad rapid strokes, as he captures a subject who looks past both him and the viewer as if amused by some private recollection.

Sometimes characterized for his use of high color and "prettified images of boneless figures," Sully achieves in this portrait what most artists struggle with and few attain, an effective use of foreshortening.[2] As Mary Tevis idly toys with the gold chain around her neck, the viewer is captured by the movement of the arm away from the surface plane and into the space that the subject occupies. In between, the long loop of the chain she winds through her fingers hangs suspended in space. The effect is trompe l'oeil, a technique of deceiving the viewer into believing that the image lies on several planes, not just the surface of the canvas, a technique that Sully's American contemporaries and successors would develop to great effect.

[1] Alan Fern, Foreword, in *Mr. Sully Portrait Painter: The Works of Thomas Sully, 1783–1872*, ed. Monroe H. Fabian (Washington, D.C.: Smithsonian Institution Press for the National Portrait Gallery, 1983), p. 7.

[2] Jules D. Prown, *American Painting: From Its Beginning to the Armory Show* (Geneva, Switz.: Skira, 1969), p. 8.

Still Life with Vegetables and Squash Blossoms,
1828
James Peale, Philadelphia
Oil on canvas (signed on back of canvas
"Painted by James Peale /
in the 79th year of his age 1828")
H. 19³⁄₁₆", W. 25³⁄₈"
57.625 Bequest of H. F. du Pont

Painted in 1828, nearly at the end of James
Peale's life, *Still Life with Vegetables and
Squash Blossoms* exudes the freshness of the
garden as specimens are arranged on a narrow
shelf in the early morning light.

A wide variety of fruits and vegetables
was readily available in the Philadelphia
markets and in the gardens that surrounded
the nearby country houses when James Peale
arranged this composition. He painted two
nearly identical versions, one that is dated

1826, and this one, dated two years later. Peale
appears to have approached this version anew.
It clearly bears the underlying drawing with
corrections that is part of the artist's initial
steps in design and execution and an
indication that the artist, never satisfied with
his work, continues to improve and refine his
pursuit of an idea.

The Brigand Alarmed, 1832
Samuel Finley Breese Morse, Italy
Oil on canvas (unsigned); H. 30", W. 25"
91.38

When Morse traveled to Rome he had a mission. He was an established artist and teacher in pursuit of his own personal definition of what art should be. In *Brigand Alarmed* Morse has combined the rich palette of Titian and the Italian masters, the classical line and postures of the French academics, and the dramatic juxtapositions of the German romantics.

Painted in the rich, warm colors of the late afternoon, *Brigand Alarmed* portrays an incident on the road from Rome to Naples. A *contadina*, or peasant girl, is standing at the entrance to the cave where a bearded highwayman is taking refuge. She warns him to be silent as soldiers representing the power of the papal armies ascend the rocky path to their location. Clearly, the artist's sympathies are on the side of the hunted.

Described in its day as allegorical genre, *Brigand Alarmed* as well as others painted by Morse on his Italian trip was exhibited at the 1833 annual exhibition of the National Academy of Design in New York, where it received high praise. The painting remained in the private collection of Dr. David Hosack until his death in 1835, when it was bequeathed to the American Art Union. It was regularly exhibited until 1849 and was then raffled off. It may have been put into its present frame at that time. The frame bears a label of the American Art Union in use at the time of the raffle. Miss L. P. Austin of Catskill, New York, was the winner of the raffle; the painting descended in her family until its recent acquisition.

Harlem, the Country House of Dr. Edmondson, Baltimore, 1834
Nicolino V. Calyo, Baltimore
Gouache on paper (unsigned, but
documented by a receipted bill of 1834)
H. 16¾", W. 29⅞"
68.60 Gift of H. F. du Pont

The beauty of the American wilderness and a European curiosity about the emerging American scene were among the reasons why numbers of topographical and landscape painters began to travel to the United States in the late eighteenth and the early nineteenth centuries. The Italian painter Nicolino Calyo came to Baltimore in 1834 and stayed for one year. During that time he painted Harlem, which is located just outside the city of Baltimore. Edmondson, the son of a wealthy Baltimore merchant, had an avid interest in horticulture and the arts. He collected paintings by American artists. Calyo chose gouache, or body color, as his medium. It is a dense form of watercolors, primarily pigment held together with a water-soluble sizing. The density of this medium makes it easier to control, and the artist is able to capture exquisite detail that is otherwise impossible with more fluid forms of watercolors.

Calyo's portrait of the house offers an incredibly complete record. We can see clearly the architectural details of both the house and its surrounding structures. The vegetation is sufficiently accurate as to be botanically identifiable. Outside the two-story orangery at the left, aloe, cactus, and other potted plants are arranged for the summer. The rear veranda of the house is shaded against the west sun, and garden sculptures fill the lawn between the house and the gazebo built above the icehouse. In the foreground a servant brings iced drinks to Edmondson and his guests. In this painting the artist preserves not just a portrait of the house but an image of a way of life.

To the Merchants of Boston this View of the LIGHT HOUSE is most humbly presented By their Humble Ser.t W.m Burgis

View of the Lighthouse, 1729
William Burgis, Boston
Mezzotint printed on laid paper (signed
on plate lower right "WBurgis del. & c. fecit")
H. 8¹³⁄₁₆", W. 12⅛"
90.74

There is some question as to where and from whom William Burgis learned the technique of mezzotint. His teacher may have been the London-trained Peter Pelham or he may have become familiar with the technique before he left England for America around 1716. Since the Restoration of Charles II, mezzotint engraving had gained in popularity to become the dominant technique in the British printmaking industry. Relying on subtle variations of tone instead of the crisp coolness of the engraved line, mezzotint well suited the imitation of portrait painting, then the major focus of British art.

First introduced by Ludwig von Siegen in the 1640s, mezzotint captured the imagination of amateurs and professionals alike. The necessary materials include a highly polished copperplate, a roughing instrument called a roulette or rocker, and a scraper. The method is to use this instrument to roughen up the copperplate in those areas where the engraver wants texture and tone. Ink sticks to the roughened areas of the copperplate and can be transferred from the plate to paper in an intaglio or rolling press. With the growth of the industry in Britain and improvements in the use of the rocker, a London engraver could secure a finely preroughened copperplate and use the scraper to pare the rough areas to minimize the amount of ink the plate would take in that area. The engraver, like the sculptor, literally cut away the highlights and lighter tones of his design from the plate.

It was a different matter in Boston in the 1720s. Without assistants or suppliers Burgis executed the coarsely laid mezzotint ground himself. From this he scraped away the highlights and diminished tones. Using strong tonal variation, Burgis succeeds in moving the viewer's eye from the choppy dark waters of the sound past the lighthouse and to the distant shores.

From a historical point Burgis's choice of the Boston lighthouse as a subject is remarkable. Located on the southernmost point of Great Braewer's Island, renamed Beacon Island in 1715, the lighthouse was the first to be built in America. The boat with cannon and crew, believed to be the *Province Galley*, was all that there was of a Massachusetts navy in 1729.

Although Burgis is recognized for designing and publishing great prospects of Boston and New York and an early view of Harvard College, this is the only one of his copperplates that he signed as both artist and engraver. As such it remains a testament to the artist-engraver's satisfaction with his work, and it becomes *the* vehicle for assessing authorship of his later mezzotint of Fort George in New York.

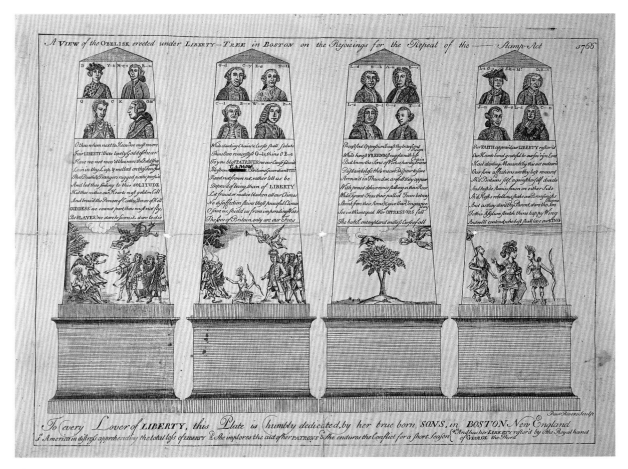

A View of the Obelisk . . ., 1766
Paul Revere, designer and engraver, Boston
Line engraving and etching printed on laid
paper (signed on plate lower right of image
"Paul Revere Sculp"); H. 10¾", W. 15¼"
92.20

Great illuminations of events of the
seventeenth and eighteenth centuries were
meant to be splendid and momentary. The
repeal of the Stamp Act was reason to
celebrate in Boston in May 1766. In
preparation for the evening's events, Paul
Revere engraved a copperplate with all four
faces of the great obelisk that was to be built
and illuminated from within. At its top were
portraits of those whom Boston patriots
recognized as supportive of their rights as
free Englishmen. In four tableaux below,
significant events relating to the Stamp Act
were depicted: the imposition of the tax by
George III's ministers under the guidance of
the devil; the protests of the colonists;
the enlightenment of George III guided by
Fame; and the reconciliation of America
with Britannia.

Revere gave notice to Bostonians that this
engraving was for sale on May 18. How many
were printed and how many were sold is
unknown. Only three impressions exist
today; on each, the hand-printed name of
"Cambden" is substituted for the engraved
name of Temple, proof that in those turbulent
times, as now, authorities were speedily
removed from public favor at any sign
of betrayal.

Revere is known for adapting previously
published satires for his own purposes. When
he is original, as in *View of the Obelisk*,
Revere's strength is to be found in the clarity
and easy readability of his work. It is the
precursor to today's editorial cartoons.

Trade card, ca. 1768
James Smither, engraver
Philadelphia
Line etching printed on laid paper (signed on
plate lower right "JS"); H. 10⅞", W. 8⅜"
60.729b

The wealth and sophistication of Philadelphia
as well as its position as the largest English-
speaking city outside of London proved
to be particularly attractive to a number of
engravers interested in leaving the competition in England. In this trade card for
Robert Kennedy, the elegant sweeps of foliage
and scrolls provided immediate reference to
the current taste, the quality of product, and
the level of personal service that a patron
could expect to find in the establishment. In
every way the label underscores Kennedy's
constant claim to provide Philadelphians with
the very best that could be obtained.

Known only by this impression, the
trade card is based on London prototypes.
With its elaborate, asymmetrical cartouche, it
is the essence of the newly introduced rococo
style. Although such trade cards tend to
survive because they were attached to objects
framed or sold, they were also suitable
for distribution to potential customers as
advertising handouts or broadsides.

Ariadne Asleep on the Island of Naxos, 1835
Asher Brown Durand, New York
Line engraving and etching, printed
on wove paper
H. 16¹⁵⁄₁₆", W. 20¼"
94.37

At its best, engraving can be equated with sculpture. In the process of engraving, an image is created by gouging out from a copper plate a pattern of lines that swell and diminish, contract and expand, as though following the surface of the object they are depicting. In the hands of a master the effect is both dramatic and plastic. When the copperplate is inked and printed onto a sheet of paper, the energies of the engraving process become graceful, sometimes forceful lines that rise slightly above the overall surface of the paper.

Durand achieved his highest level of success as an engraver in translating John Vanderlyn's enormous oil painting *Ariadne Asleep on the Island of Naxos* into an engraving. First exhibited in Paris to wide acclaim, the painting was brought back to America only to be scorned for the nakedness of its subject. It remained stored in Vanderlyn's studio until Durand bought it with the ultimate purpose of making an engraving. Durand began by preparing a study of the painting in full color but in the scale of the intended engraving. This small version served as the model.

There are seven extant working states, proofs pulled from the copperplate at intervals as the work progressed. This number is more than we have for any other American line engraving of the early nineteenth century. Although state six is missing from this set, the six working proofs and open letter state, as a body, give great insight into Durand's methods of working. With so large a copperplate, and one very difficult to print, the engraver's efforts were never adequately compensated. It is, however, a brilliant achievement in American printmaking, recognized in its own day as now, a masterpiece.

BOOKS AND MANUSCRIPTS

The Winterthur library collections hold more than 500,000 books, manuscripts, periodicals, prints, photographs, and related materials. The challenge of identifying masterworks from these was formidable and raised a multitude of questions for the library's curators. Can an object that is a multiple be a masterpiece? What are the relative importance of physical form and intellectual content? How vital are subject matter and intent? What role does superior craftsmanship play? And, for I must admit that we all have our favorites, how valid is a curator's own affection for a particular book? In the end, we chose our masterworks from among the library's many illustrated books and manuscripts. These are collections of great depth and interest, particularly for their holdings of eighteenth- and nineteenth-century materials and for their representation of varied graphic and manuscript techniques. The items we chose all meet certain criteria: visual beauty; excellence in materials, craftsmanship, and state of preservation; appropriate method of illustration; relevance to the focus of the museum's other collections; and intellectual interest.

From this list, the primary criterion was visual beauty. The means to achieving this end differs in each chosen item but implies in all the presence of superior workmanship in the creation of the object, high quality materials (paper, ink, binding), and the good fortune in having been preserved in excellent condition, for books and manuscripts are particularly susceptible to ill-treatment through heat and cold, dampness and aridity, and mishandling by readers.

Visual beauty is in the eye of the beholder, and such judgments are always subjective. There are, however, certain undeniable qualities these articles all exhibit in their illustrations: glowing color and a choice of graphic technique that is suitable to the subject matter. The mezzotint plate of tulips from the *Temple of Flora* perfectly exemplifies these qualities: the velvety texture of the graphic image conveys the softness of the flowers and at the same time allows for the full

131

brilliance of their coloring to be reproduced. By contrast, the freshness of the watercolors of the Pennsylvania countryside from John Lewis Krimmel's manuscript sketchbook suggests their creation as quick records of scenery made on the spot. Each of the other books and manuscripts exhibits a similarly high standard in conception and workmanship. Because the illustrations were created by a variety of methods, including watercolor, lithography, and engraving, they afford the viewer a sense of the range of techniques available for luxury book illustration during their period.

In addition to forming parts of a major collecting focus for the library, these books and manuscripts are all relevant to Winterthur's other collections and areas of interest, whether it be garden history, the history of graphic arts and techniques and design, the visual recording of daily life in early America and its perception by foreign travelers, or the material surroundings of households of the period. The library has always existed to further the work of the museum and of the graduate programs associated with it, and these documents and the many others we hold were all acquired for that purpose. Each of them is far more than just a pretty face!

The books and manuscripts selected each have their own intellectual significance for the history of the arts and associated trades and crafts. Sir William Hamilton's catalogue of his collection of Greek vases is a key document in the development of the neoclassical style, its plates having been seen and copied by the potter Josiah Wedgwood—while still in page proof—and thus disseminated in multiple on a grand scale. The plates of personal and household goods in the French tradesman's catalogue furnish a detailed visual record of the range of consumer choice at a particular place and point in time. The catalogue is as well an important document for the history of trade.

There is, to me, one further quality that sets each of these books and manuscripts apart and may well be the one factor that in the end makes them so superior. They were all—even the anonymous French tradesman's catalogue—creations of affection by their makers, in some cases amounting to obsession. It is this affection that focused such painstaking care on them from concept to realization. Although their production may have caused financial ruin for some, these works of art were a labor of love; authors considered it money well spent in pursuit of an ideal well achieved. This quality, which resides in each of these works, reaches out to the viewer still.

In sum, an object that is a multiple can indeed be a masterwork, as we see in the choices discussed here. Physical form, particularly when enhanced by superior craftsmanship and fine materials, is an important standard of excellence. The appeal of such objects increases when the subject matter is intellectually significant. Each book and manuscript projects a sense of discovery, one that illumines even the everyday and enlarges our understanding of the times in which they were created. Their complexity invites us to return to them for further exploration. And yes, our own affection for a particular book or manuscript is just as valid a criterion as all others mentioned. It is the link between ourselves—the readers—and the books' creators.

Lehigh River, Pennsylvania,
Sunday, September 5, 1813
John Lewis Krimmel
Watercolor over pencil
H. 4⁹⁄₁₆", W. 8⅞"
59 X 5.1

John Lewis Krimmel's story is one of promise
cut short. Born in Württemberg, Germany,
in 1786, he emigrated to Philadelphia in 1809,
joining an older brother there. Krimmel
immediately entered into the artistic life of
the city and began to produce the paintings,
such as Winterthur's *Quilting Frolic* (1813),
that have led him to be considered America's
first genre painter. The painter's sketchbooks
testify to his fascination with the everyday life

and landscape of young America. They are
one of the library's great treasures. The four
pencil and watercolor sketches shown here
date from 1813 to 1820. Krimmel seems to have
been charmed by the freshness of the
American landscape and its inhabitants, both
animal—he apparently shared Benjamin
Franklin's opinion of the nobility of our
native turkey—and human. Many of his
sketches illustrate everyday domestic artifacts,
such as spinning wheels. Tragically, he died in
a drowning accident in Germantown,
Pennsylvania, in 1821, thus cutting short
the development of a still-refining and
maturing talent.

Landscape, Tuesday, September 7, 1813
John Lewis Krimmel
Watercolor and ink over pencil
H. 4⁹⁄₁₆", W. 8⅞"
59 x 5.1

Spinning wheels, Saturday, July 10, 1819
John Lewis Krimmel
Watercolor over pencil; H. 4¼", W. 6⁷⁄₁₆"
59 x 5.6

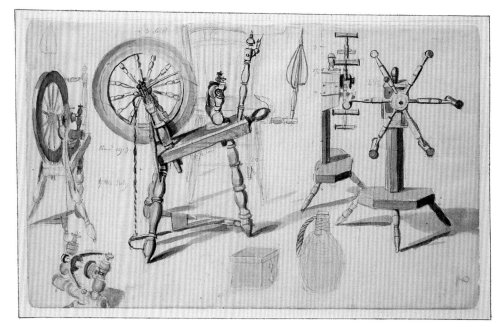

Turkeys, ca. 1819–20
John Lewis Krimmel
Watercolor over pencil
H. 5", W. 7 "
59 X 5.7

Chariot scene
Hand-colored engraving, F. A. David
From Pierre-François Hugues d'Hancarville,
Collection of Etruscan, Greek, and Roman
Antiquities from the Cabinet of the Honble.
Wm. Hamilton . . . , 4 vols. (Naples: F.
Morelli, 1766–67), 3: pl. 52
Page: H. 18¼", W. 14"

Gift of the Friends of Winterthur

Sir William Hamilton's posting to the court of
Naples in 1764 afforded this cultivated
Englishman an unparalleled opportunity to
form an impressive collection of the
antiquities then being excavated in Italy. The
collection, primarily of vases, was sold by
Hamilton to the British Museum and was a
major influence on late eighteenth-century
and early nineteenth-century artists and
designers such as John Flaxman and Josiah
Wedgwood. This catalogue of the collection,
lavishly documented by the text of French
art historian P. F. H. d'Hancarville (1719–1805)
and the black and white and hand-colored
engravings of F. A. David, reputedly cost
Hamilton £6,000 to produce, an under-
standable figure in view of the handsome
result. In this plate from the third of four
volumes, d'Hancarville speculates that the
scene depicts the hero Ulysses mounting his
war chariot, preceded by his herald, followed
by a page, and accompanied by a poet,
chanter of songs of victory in battle.

Footwear
Watercolor drawings
From a catalogue of watercolors depicting
French wares (France, ca. 1810)
Page: H. 16", W. 11"
64 x 68.2 Gift of the Friends of Winterthur

The library's two volumes of drawings of
household objects and items of clothing are
among the most captivating of all our
holdings. Because they lack text, date,
ownership marks, or other clues, these
volumes have remained enigmas that
challenge today's researchers. Recent French
scholarship on similar documents has
established that these compilations of
watercolors were produced during the early
nineteenth century and were possibly used by
wholesalers or middlemen as catalogues of
available goods for their retailer clients. Very
likely the goods they advertise were aimed at
an expanding middle-class consumer market
and were produced by Parisian artisans and
craftsmen. However, none of this explains
the care that went into producing these
drawings. They are examples of craftsmanship that transcend necessity; the result is
a masterpiece.

Classical profile
Hand-colored mezzotint,
after a chalk drawing by Giles Hussey
From Francis Webb, *Panharmonicon*
(London, 1815), facing p. 10
Page: H. 11⅝", W. 9¼"
RBR NC65 W36 Waldron Phoenix
Belknap, Jr., Fund purchase

Panharmonicon is a tribute to the unlikely friendship between an eccentric expatriate English painter, Giles Hussey (1710–88), and Francis Webb (1735–1815), a nonconformist minister, minor bureaucrat, and political writer. Hussey's undeniable talent was thwarted by his own adherence to the cause of the exiled Stuart claimants to the English throne, whom he had met while studying in Italy, and by an unwillingness to cultivate patronage on his return to England. He died a religious recluse. After Hussey's death, Webb championed his theory of harmonic proportion in the representation of the human body, based on an elaborate mathematical scheme. This plate is a reproduction of one of the chalk drawings for which Hussey was especially noted. It is a mezzotint *a la poupée* (in color), enhanced by hand coloring in the details of the face and hair. An understanding of Hussey's theories is unnecessary to appreciate this handsome example of neoclassical drawing.

Spring
Aquatint, W. J. Bennett,
after a watercolor by George Harvey
From George Harvey, *Harvey's Scenes of the
Primitive Forest of America . . .* (London: By
the author, 1841), no. 2
Image: H. 14", W. 10⁷⁄₁₆"

George Harvey (1801–78) was one of many
English and European artists who visited this
country, were captivated by its scenery, and
attempted to record their impressions for their
compatriots. While supporting himself as a
painter of miniatures, Harvey began his

ambitious attempt to record the American
landscape in every weather and every time of
day; the result was a series of watercolors
intended to be issued as aquatints with
explanatory text. Harvey planned to release
these through subscription in parts over a span
of time, as Audubon had done with his bird and
animal prints. Financial problems intervened,
however, and only the four scenes in this
portfolio were ever published. The Winterthur
library holds the London edition; the work also
appeared in New York at the same time. *Spring*
shows a scene very typical of an era in which
land was rapidly being cleared for an expanding

population. Scholars have noted that the
clearing of forests, like the appearance of
railroad lines, was an unambiguous sign of
progress to audiences of the nineteenth century.

As each individual Tulip shew
display of the wonderful powe
before us, for our recreation,
the colouring ingredients, so
of each petal! How much
ravishing beauties of the

The most
require our
the several s

Most
Louis X
majesty,
It finely
and th
border
nam
TI
pe
o

Tulips

London, Published Aug.t 1st 1798, by D.r Thornton

Ranagle pinx.t

Earlom sculp.t

Tulips
Hand-colored mezzotint, Richard Earlom,
after a painting by Philip Reinagle
From Robert John Thornton, *New Illustration
of the Sexual System of Carolus von Linnaeus . . .
and the Temple of Flora . . . Being Picturesque,
Botanical, Coloured Plates of Selected Plants . . .
with Descriptions* (London: By the author, 1807)
Page: H. 22⅛", W. 17⅛"
RBR QK92 T51 PFF Gift of the
Friends of Winterthur

The *Temple of Flora* is justly known as one of
the most magnificent flower books ever
published. It was intended to illustrate the
then-revolutionary Linnaean system of
botanical classification and reflects as well the
era's fascination with the discovery and
classification of exotic plants. The creation of
this book was the lifelong obsession of Robert
Thornton (1768?–1837) and his financial ruin,
but it has assured his posthumous fame. The
flower plates he commissioned from a
number of artists and engravers were
deliberately meant to display a variety of plant
forms and to include backgrounds intended to
suggest the plants' varied and often romantic
countries of origin (as the windmill here
implies Holland). The artist, Philip Reinagle,
and the engraver, Richard Earlom, have
together produced in the mezzotint *Tulips* one
of the most luscious of botanical illustrations.
The three-dimensional quality of the flowers
was achieved by color printing in brown and
blue and then by hand-coloring.

Eye for Excellence: Masterworks from Winterthur

Editor: Onie Rollins

Copy Editor: Teresa A. Vivolo

Typefaces: Adobe Minion and Trajan

Paper: Warren Lustro Dull, 80 lb. text

Designed by Staples & Charles Ltd/Adam Cohn

Typesetting by General Typographers, Inc.

Printed by The Stinehour Press